A QUEST FOR EXCELLENCE

A QUEST FOR EXCELLENCE

Building High Performance NGOs

REHEMA C. BATTI

ISBN-13: 9781523964345

ISBN-10: 1523964340

To individuals committed to building stronger civic infrastructure by bringing transformational change within NGOs

ACKNOWLEDGEMENTS

The writing of this book would not have been possible without the amazing support received from my husband Dr. Samoel Khamadi and children Natasha, Hope, and Zawadi Ashimosi. Thanks for making me appreciate the value of leading a balanced life.

Special thanks to my mother Catherine Batti for her encouragement and prayers.My appreciation also goes to my siblings and their families for their support.

The content of this book was inspired by local NGOs in the field of development, dedicated NGO staff and professional colleagues, who, work tirelessly to bring services closer to communities. They continuously search for innovative ways to ensure NGOs attain sustainable growth and performance.

My appreciation also goes to the staff team from CreateSpace Publishing for their contribution in editing and designing this book.

ADDITIONAL BOOKS DONE BY AUTHOR

1. *Strengthening Local NGOs Internal Capacity: Experiences from the Field*
2. *Community-Based Partnerships: Nurturing Strategic NGO Collaboration*

TABLE OF CONTENTS

PREFACE

High-performance NGOs are fundamental in promoting developmental change that brings lasting transformational impact at community level.

Local NGOs have to compete for survival through projects; therefore, they are continuously required to review and adopt management approaches that give them a competitive advantage. What practices do NGOs adopt, to demonstrate that they are high-performance organizations with sustainable structures?

There is a need to redesign organizations through building new capabilities and adopting practices that will lead to transformational change and sustain high performance. Focusing only on developing projects without institutionalizing management practices that enhance the competitiveness of an NGO will eventually lead to failure. This book is divided into the following chapters:

Chapter One gives an overview of leadership concepts and practice, highlights some leadership theories, and briefly explores some strategic leadership management practices required in NGOs.

Chapter Two looks at the categories of knowledge and the principles that guide knowledge management. Even though knowledge is an important asset very few local NGOs are able to harness or utilize this asset effectively to improve performance. The chapter also highlights the value of managing knowledge within an organization to increase an NGO's competitive advantage and improve performance.

Chapter Three highlights how NGOs can utilize communication practices and tools to manage performance and their relations with both internal and external stakeholders. The chapter emphasizes the importance of building an NGO's communication capacities.

Chapter Four sets out to discuss the need for an entrepreneurial approach in managing NGOs. New attitudes and competencies need to be effectively explored and embraced so that NGOs operate in more innovative ways through exploiting viable opportunities in their sector.

Chapter Five this chapter highlights some key board aspects, the importance of the board, and its functions. Managing NGOs requires effective governance structures. The question that comes to mind is, to what extent are governance structures fulfilling their strategic role to promote NGO performance and growth? This is an area that most local NGOs and donors have given minimal emphasis, yet it has a great impact on the development and performance of an NGO.

Chapter Six highlights sustainability management practices that NGOs can use to strengthen and improve performance and viability. Local NGOs in Africa and other developing nations are grappling with issues of sustainability. For many NGOs, once external funding ends, some activities come to a halt, and eventually the entire organization closes. What makes an organization continue to grow and provide competitive services ten years after its initiation?

Chapter Seven concludes the book by highlighting how NGOs can progress toward being high-performance organizations. Many local NGOs are losing their competitive advantage because they have inadequate organizational practices that assist them achieve consistent and sustained NGO performance or growth.

This book will benefit nonprofit organization staff, development workers, board members and leaders of community-based organizations in the field of development who desire to see organizations achieve sustained growth. Students studying NGO management will find this book beneficial as it provides an insightful look into aspects that create high-performance NGOs.

This book will benefit Organization Development and Change Management professionals involved in designing improvement programs within NGOs.

INTRODUCTION

Local NGOs of different sizes and operating in diverse communities, must find innovative tactics to help nurture the growth and performance of the organization to meet the demands of their stakeholders. The development field is complex and dynamic, and there is need to understand what makes NGOs effective, competitive, and feasible within their contexts of operation.

Local NGOs are grassroots organizations that normally have fewer formal structures or operations, and they grow or expand when the prevailing conditions are supportive. Local NGOs operate in remote areas with poor infrastructure, and this means development work is often dynamic and complex.

NGOs thrive when they have resources that enable them to achieve the mission of the organization, and yet they sometimes struggle with barriers or limitations that hinder consistent growth, effectiveness, and sustainability.

Malena[1] notes that NGOs often face barriers such as limited financial and management expertise, limited institutional capacity, low levels of self-sustainability, inadequate or isolated inter-organizational communication, and lack of understanding of the broader social or economic context.

Some of these obstacles have resulted in poor performance among local NGOs causing them to lose credibility among stakeholders, or it has resulted in the decline of an organization's project resources.

This book is about how local NGOs can grow into high performance organizations. The book is based on the author's experience working with local NGOs and learning about factors that nurture a highly competitive organization.

Many local NGOs depend on projects they undertake that are tied to time and funding stipulated by the donors. Therefore, it has become imperative that organizations have in place skilled leadership, effective knowledge management practices, a strong reputation, effective governance systems and sustainability management practices for them to be effective.

The aim of the book is not to present prescriptive solutions on how an NGO can consistently ensure sustained growth to become a high-performance organization.

However, the author would like to share with those working with and those interested in working with local NGOs some experiences and gaps so that together with others, they can adequately support local NGOs in reaching their potential through meeting their envisioned mandates within their contexts.

An organization's internal and external context has been observed to influence the ability of the NGO to achieve sustained performance. The presence of strategic leadership, knowledge management practices, corporate communication, effective governance, entrepreneurial spirit, and organizational sustainability practices are becoming crucial practices within local NGOs.

Strategic leadership and effective governance skills are required for coordinating available NGO resources to achieve change or success. The expertise and competencies of employees are important resources that need to be harnessed and utilized effectively through knowledge management.

An NGO's reputation and brand are key tools that promote its competitive advantage and sustainability in the marketplace. Local NGOs are currently being challenged to strengthen their relations with other NGOs, the business sector, the government, and local communities.

This requires an organization to embrace corporate communication practices that help nurture its relations with stakeholders. Organizational communication plays an important role in assisting an NGO build its image and in executing the organization's strategic initiatives.

The presence of a growing, highly competitive and dynamic environment in many countries requires an NGO to adopt an entrepreneurial spirit so that it can seize opportunities provided within its external environment.

OVERVIEW OF HIGH PERFORMANCE NGOs

The most complex management task is to promote innovative ideas that will provide a sense of direction and creativity aimed at identifying new opportunities and creating new business models. NGOs that desire to excel need to meet the demands for innovation, technological changes and production of quality services.

Local NGOs are important players in the development sector in many developing countries. However, most local NGOs fail to proactively identify and seize opportunities that will give them a competitive edge.

Why do many local NGOs fail to consistently sustain high performance? This can be attributed to the fact that many are poorly managed and led by individuals with inadequate management and leadership competencies resulting in stagnation and poor performance. In addition, many local NGOs fail to readjust and realign their operational practices to improve their performance and survival.

A high performance NGO can be described as an organization that consistently achieves outstanding results and sustainable growth compared to its peers in the same sector over an extended period of time.

In the past, success and sustainable growth have been elusive elements among most NGOs due to underdeveloped management practices. For example, it is interesting to observe that an NGO may have dedicated and qualified workforce but fail to harness the full potential of this asset due to outdated organizational design or structure, and poor leadership practices.

In other scenarios, it is unfortunate to note that despite the fact that stakeholders', priorities have changed as they always will, many NGOs sometimes fail to recognize this and continue to use outdated strategies that no longer meet stakeholders' expectations.

This book is intended to highlight practices to help facilitate a better understanding of management practices and presents ideas that can contribute to the creation of highly competitive local NGOs.

A high performing NGO has the capacity to adapt and be responsive to changes in its internal and external environments. The organization continuously improves its core competencies, has an empowered and professional workforce, and has the capacity to sustain performance over time. In addition, there is alignment between strategy and performance through the adoption of competitive strategies.

Three aspects that affect an organization's ability to sustain high performance are: senior management with an inaccurate understanding of the marketplace in which the organization operates, leadership and workforce behaviors are not in alignment with stakeholder and marketplace expectations, and, organization systems and processes do not support the organization's vision and strategy.[2]

The effectiveness of local NGOs in the development sector is dependent on the adoption of organizational practices that enhance their performance and sustainability. The author shares some practices that can assist an NGO in its pursuit to becoming a high performance organization.

In many local NGOs, some practices discussed in this book are being partially implemented or not practiced at all. Some practices tend to be undertaken in an ad-hoc manner depending on the leadership or prevailing culture within the organization.

The thoughts shared in this book emphasize the need to have responsive structures and consistent practices to enable local NGOs to make a difference.

A local NGO's ability to be responsive to changing dynamics in its operating environment is a must in the development sector. When effective organizational practices are incorporated into local NGOs they can minimize failure, especially in the early and later years.

This book does not cover all aspects or factors that will enable a local NGO to achieve high performance. The message presented is that building a high performance NGO is determined or influenced by many factors and some of which are covered in this book.

This book aims to challenge and give readers an opportunity to explore factors that impact on high performance among local NGOs based on perspectives shared in this book and the reader's own experiences.

Chapter 1

STRATEGIC LEADERSHIP IN NGOs

Local NGO leaders are faced with complex challenges as they lead organizations both at the personal and organizational levels. Many local NGOs face internal management challenges that result in a weak governing structure, a nonoperational strategic plan, diminishing resources, inadequate staff capacity, failed change management programs, and the decline of the NGO's performance. These limitations can sometimes be linked to unsustainable leadership practices.

An NGO requires leaders who have the commitment and capacity to review NGO business processes, identify those that are not effective and then propose and implement processes that will ensure the organization continues to grow into a high performance NGO.

Strategic leadership is a process that involves leading a team or organization toward its goal. Local NGOs are in need of strategic leaders who support the organization to gain a competitive advantage in a dynamic market.

Strategic leadership is, therefore, becoming a crucial management aspect that can assist local NGOs improve performance and sustained growth. Strategic leadership transforms an organization's hidden potential to enable it to seize opportunities that exist in the environment.

OVERVIEW OF LEADERSHIP CONCEPTS

Leadership is crucial and is one of the significant contributors to an organization's sustained performance. Leadership failure is not a new phenomenon and is a common occurrence, even at well-performing companies. Leadership is seen to directly affect organization climate and culture.

Leadership is a process and not a person. It is dynamic and context specific and leaders are ideally expected to lead more and manage less. But this is not the case in many local NGOs.

Strategic leadership requires one to think, act decisively and influence others in ways that ensure sustainable success for the organization.[3]

However, this kind of leadership does not come easily in most local NGOs and very few leaders exhibit any strategic skills. Yet these skills are necessary during growth and when resources are tight to ensure focused distribution and focus in the appropriate areas.

Organizational leaders and managers positioned at different levels make the difference between failure and the successful achievement of an NGO's strategic goals. How leaders determine strategic actions and mobilize others to implement them is critical to any organization's performance and continued survival.

I. DIFFERENCES IN LEADERSHIP AND MANAGEMENT

Leadership and management both involve mobilizing, influencing and working with people for effective organization management. Leaders alternate between a broad range of behaviors to the changing demands of innovation and context. Leadership and management when viewed from an organizational performance point have some distinct perspectives.

Leadership (doing the right things):

    i. Aligns people with the vision
   ii. Motivates, inspires and energizes followers
  iii. Champions organizational change
  iv. Empowers others to cope with change
   v. Provides meaningful direction to collective effort

vi. Causes deliberate effort to achieve purpose
vii. Communicates vision and direction

Management (doing things right):

i.   Communicates tasks and deliverables
ii.   Ensures a degree of order and consistency
iii. Analyzes and solves problems
iv.   Supervises and organizes staff
v.   Develops plans and budgets
vi.   Measures and reports activity progress
vii. Handle project and team complexity

Organizations that fail to see the differences between the two are bound to decline in performance no matter how well they are managed. However, for an NGO to consistently improve its performance there is a need for managers to demonstrate leadership skills and for leaders to equally display some managerial skills.

Attitudes, perceptions, and understanding of, leadership have evolved over the years. It is now recognized that ineffective management and unethical behavior among leaders can threaten the performance, legitimacy, and sustainability of any organization. This emphasizes the need to have relevant leadership capabilities when leading NGOs.

II. LEADERSHIP THEORIES

Leadership is context specific, and its authority is derived from personality, knowledge, and position. The following are some leadership theories;

i. GREAT MAN THEORY

This theory supposes that leaders are simply born with the required internal social skills, intelligence, and confidence. It states that leaders are naturally born, not made.

ii. TRAIT THEORY

This theory argues that a person can inherit certain leadership qualities and traits that are needed for leadership roles. The theory lists personality characteristics that are observed among leaders.

iii. BEHAVIORAL THEORY

This theory's focus is on the premise that being a leader is not an inborn characteristic. The argument in this theory is that a person can learn to be a leader through observation and training.

iv. PARTICIPATIVE LEADERSHIP THEORY

According to the participative leadership theory, the leader takes the ideas and proposals of others into consideration. The leader encourages contributions and involvement from individuals and helps members feel important.

v. SITUATIONAL THEORY

The theory argues that a person or leader chooses an action based on the context at a given time. The way the leader responds is based on factors like the expertise of employees, prevailing forces within the organization or situation. This leadership is highly variable and is based on the maturity of the team or individuals being led, the task to be accomplished, and the structure of the organization.

For example, the Hersey-Blanchard situational leadership theory emphasizes matching leadership approach with individual or group maturity and specified tasks.

vi. CONTINGENCY THEORY

The theory stresses that different styles suit different situations or environments. It argues that successful leadership is dependent upon factors such as qualities of followers, leadership styles, and contexts of the situations.

vii. TRANSACTIONAL THEORY

The theory focuses on organization, supervision, and group performance. Its focus is on providing rewards and punishments. The theory suggests that when there are clear structures in an organization, leadership will work effectively.

viii. TRANSFORMATIONAL THEORY

This theory is also termed as relationship theory and focuses on the interactions between leaders and followers. The assumption is that individuals will go along with, imitate or respect a person who inspires or motivates them.

Transformational leaders inspire and motivate individuals or teams to see the higher good of the organization. They set the pace in terms of developing the vision and focus of the organization and show by their attitudes and actions what they expect from others.

They have a strong commitment toward attaining the organization's goals, and this serves to support others in the organization to move forward. They build passion and energy within teams and are culture creators.

III. LEADERSHIP APPROACHES AND CHARACTERISTICS

The leadership style of a leader defines an organization, and this means if an NGO is to be committed to its mission and values, the leadership style has to align with the values it seeks to uphold. For example, a democratic leader in a bureaucratic organization will create chaos, or an autocratic leader in a coalition structure will fail or cause frustration among team members.

A leadership style refers to behaviors that an individual in a leadership position exhibits as he or she coordinates, guides, and manages teams within an organization. A few leadership approaches are discussed here; however, the list is not exhaustive, as new leadership styles emerge as organizational structures and dynamics continue to evolve.

i. AUTHORITARIAN LEADERSHIP

It is also known as autocratic leadership, where the leader's focus is to ensure tasks are accomplished. The leader controls all the decisions, goals, or tasks that are to be undertaken within the organization. This leadership style is all about discipline, control, and organization.

Focus is on the work to be done, and the leader makes decisions based on his or her own ideas or perceptions without consulting others. It gives rise to a sense that other team members are not trusted with tasks or decisions. This leadership style can affect staff morale, as there are minimal empowerment strategies present.

This style is, however, useful when there is a need for tasks to be completed within a short timeframe, or an individual staff competency is low on a particular task or skills are in short supply, and there is need to set clear tasks to assist the organization achieve its goals.

ii. PATERNALISTIC LEADERSHIP

The leader combines work-centered behavior with a parental- protective-centered concern for employees. It can be viewed as a dictatorial leadership style.

It has a fatherly style of interaction with the others in the work environment or sometimes the leader is perceived as an expert father and exerts his or her power in the organization.

Employees are shaped and work is crafted based on the leader's beliefs and values. This leadership style may be found in an organization with a hierarchical structure and is based on a reward system. The challenge with this style is that the leader eventually starts having favorites among the employees who seem to be loyal and considers their input more than that from others.

This style can lead to more dependence on the leadership and the need for more supervision. It often results in low staff morale especially for those who are not recognized or feel undervalued (as they are viewed to have a minimal loyal connection to management).

iii. PARTICIPATIVE LEADERSHIP

It is a people-oriented or democratic style of leadership, and the leader's focus is on people and work. The leader tries to motivate individuals and teams to play an active role in assuming control of their work and to give input on objectives to be achieved.

This style of leadership gives individuals a sense of purpose and value which creates a sense of belonging. It is a style that empowers and motivates individuals through involvement.

This style can lead to improvement in the quality of decisions made if the right and relevant individuals (those who have the right expertise and relevant professional experience) within the organization are engaged and consulted.

This approach also works best when individuals have an interest in the organization's mission and goals and very high levels of trust among the management team exist. However, this leadership style can discourage employees especially if the leaders ask for opinions and later do not consider them; this leads to feelings of betrayal.

iv. BUREAUCRATIC LEADERSHIP

This approach is fixed on pursuing a set of rules and focuses on the hierarchy of leadership. It is a style that is based on rules and historical procedures regardless of changes that occur in its environs. For example, all management and employee roles are structured into defined offices and positions are structured in a hierarchical manner.

The leader's approach or style of management is defined or determined by a system of behavioral rules and technical rules. The leaders derive power from managing or controlling the flow of information within the unit or organization.

The leader heavily relies on written documentation that guides how things are to be done. The leader ensures that staff follow procedures, work by the book and demands a businesslike conduct in the workplace.

This leadership approach is relevant where the work environment involves safety such as like working with complex machinery or highly toxic substances.

It is, however, not appropriate for organizations that need creativity and innovation from its workforce to expand the organization's operations.

v. LAISSEZ FAIRE LEADERSHIP

This style has a low emphasis on performance and people. It is described as an individual-centered style, and it assumes people are unpredictable and uncontrollable. The leader keeps a low profile and leaves people alone.

The leader takes little interest in managerial functions, and the teams are left on their own. The role is one of non-involvement; and the leader provides basic information, minimal supervision, and resources for the team.

This style fosters an atmosphere of minimal engagement with employees. For example, the orientation of job functions and policies are done at an employee level. The laissez-faire leader or supervisor may not provide this information and assumes that the new employee will learn from others.

This leadership style is appropriate for teams with individuals who are highly qualified and motivated self-starters. The leader tends to allow the teams to work on their own and provides minimal or no supervision. Unfortunately, it can be perceived to mean a leader is not exerting sufficient control, and, under this leadership, team roles are poorly defined and staff morale tends to be low.

Teams under such leadership lack direction, individuals blame one another for mistakes, individuals refuse to accept responsibility and show a lack of progress at work.

vi. RELATIONS- OR PEOPLE-ORIENTED LEADERSHIP

The relations-or people-oriented leadership is low on performance but high on people. The leader tends to be emotionally or socially connected with individuals on the team.

The leader trusts subordinates, feels less need to control them, avoids close supervision, maintains personal relationships, open channels of communication, and sees delegation to individuals as opportunities to tap their potential.

The leader is responsive to the demands and feelings of the group members and they are allowed more freedom and autonomy in their work. The leader focuses on coordinating and building the team.

vii. SERVANT LEADERSHIP

This type of leadership approach focuses on empowering teams through a balanced approach to handling life and work. Leaders gain authority based on the values and ideals they uphold. They desire to serve others by assisting them in achieving their goals and improving their competencies through creating enabling environments.

A servant leader has large doses of self-awareness and this helps the leader focus on serving the needs of the team and the growth of the individuals within the organization.

This style of leadership explores and understands the driving force of the team and seeks to support the team's purpose. The leader strives to understand and nurture the personal and professional growth of employees so that they are empowered enough to contribute to the overall goals of the organization.

This style recognizes the fact that individuals need to be appreciated and accepted for they possess unique skills and talents. The leader takes an interest in ideas and suggestions from the team and strives to encourage employees or members of a team in decision-making. The leader assumes that the staff have good intentions.

When making decisions, they rely greatly on the power of persuasion and not their position of influence. This means the individual is good at consensus building among team members.

Servant leadership style uses a group-oriented approach as the leader desires to promote a sense of community and shared power through inclusive decision-making processes.

The leader is convinced that the fundamental role of the organization is to create a positive impact on its workforce and stakeholders rather than focusing on only making gains. They are keen on developing trusting relationships by nurturing a collaborative spirit among teams and seeking to address the needs of the customers.

viii. CHARISMATIC LEADERSHIP

The individual has high enthusiasm and is a great motivator of people. This leadership style is based on the individual using enthusiasm to motivate or lead the team and authority is gained through social skills.

The individual assumes that charm and grace are all that is needed to create followers, motivate and inspire others. These leaders are skilled communicators and can communicate to their followers at a personal and emotional level.

This individual has great confidence in his or her followers and is very persuasive. The leader is keen on making the group very distinct, thus setting it apart from other teams by making the team believe they are superior to others. However, charismatic leaders tend to believe more in themselves than in other members of the team.

The leader attaches himself or herself firmly to the identity of the group and will sometimes take personal risks and undertake unconventional behaviors to advocate for an issue. The leader seeks to instill commitment to philosophical goals and devotion to the leader. The leader is viewed as a hero and as irreplaceable by followers but is, however, intolerant of individuals who project themselves as challengers.

This leadership style focuses on scanning the environment and discerning the moods and concerns of individuals within the team or audience. This style is most appropriate when there is low staff morale and there is need to stir the team up to become creative and passionate to achieve a new direction or mission.

ix. SITUATIONAL LEADERSHIP

This leadership style is determined by the followers or the team the individual is leading. This means the behavior of the team will guide how the leader will lead or what style to use.

This approach requires the leader to adjust to the different variables within the organization such as the maturity of employees and the work environment, among other things. It is adaptable and flexible to the situation at hand.

The leader's approach depends on the task at hand and the individual's competence to accomplish it. The behavior of the leader will motivate the team to either work or not to work.

This leader is supportive and sympathetic to the challenges the team faces as it undertakes tasks hence, the team is motivated and committed to work.

This approach puts a lot of pressure on the leader to constantly assess a situation before taking any action. This view also puts the responsibility on the leader to develop the team where there is inexperience or minimal expertise.

Unfortunately, a situational leader may be perceived as inconsistent, and the team may lose trust in the leader because of the adjustments he or she has made to fit into the situation. This leadership style is seen as dependent on the individual's personality and leadership experience or lack of experience; type of organization; and the maturity and competence of the workforce.

It is important to remember that each leadership style is best suited for a particular organization depending on the prevailing context, age, operations and mission of the organization. Therefore, organizations have to identify, select or nurture an appropriate leadership approach that will help reap maximum benefits for the organization and its employees.

LEADERSHIP ROLES AND FUNCTIONS

Strategic leaders apply approaches that are appropriate to empower the workforce and to increase the NGO's performance and competitive advantage.

It is important that local NGO leaders seek to develop their leadership skills through periodic assessment, the will to change through learning from other outstanding leaders and training to ensure they have the right leadership approach to build the NGO's competitiveness in its sector of operation.

Adair[4] highlights three broad functions of leadership:

a. Achieving the common TASK, this means if the task is not achieved the team gets frustrated.
b. Building and maintaining the TEAM, ensuring the team is held together.

   c.   Motivating and developing the INDIVIDUAL, understanding the individual.

A strategic leader's core responsibility is to influence the workforce toward the attainment of the NGO's vision and mission so as to have an impact on the organization's performance. Therefore, strategic leadership involves the following roles:

   a.   Providing purpose and vision
   b.   Involvement in strategic thinking and planning
   c.   Operational leadership and administration that inspires confidence and action
   d.   Ensuring the NGO is competitive based on organizational context
   e.   Meaningful involvement of internal and external stakeholders
   f.   Good role modeling that influences positive organizational culture

IV. THE ROLE OF POWER IN LEADERSHIP

Power is a tool in leadership and depending on how it is used it can lead to either positive or negative results within an organization. Leaders derive power from coercion, reward, expertise, charisma, and position.

a. REWARD

Power is founded on the ability of an individual to provide benefits or incentives such as job promotions, gifts, and salary increments. People comply if the reward is something valued by the targeted person. Leaders are often able to give out rewards. If people expect a reward for doing what a leader wants, there's a high probability that they will do it.

b. COERCION

It is based on the ability to administer punishments to subordinates. It involves threatening to fire, demote people, deny individuals privileges, or give them undesirable assignments to make them comply.

c. LEGITIMATE /POSITION-BASED

Power is derived from authority based on one's official title or position, for example director, ambassador or head of a department. This type of power is unstable and unpredictable, as it is tied to a post, and, unfortunately, if the individual loses the position, the power disappears since its influence is position based.

d. EXPERT

This power is based on possession of a given body of knowledge, methodologies and patterns, and/or skills. People will listen to a person with knowledge and skills who can help them understand a situation, propose solutions, and use solid judgment. Hence, the individual derives power from expertise.

e. REFERENT

Referent power comes from attraction or respect for someone. It means a person is liked and respected by another, and that individual strongly identifies with that person. For example, movie stars or celebrities have referent power.

f. ASSOCIATIVE

It is power that comes from being linked to an individual or influential organization member who has power. Individuals in leadership then exert power because they have access to the power source or can influence people with power.

The way in which leaders use their power can positively or negatively impact an NGO's performance and its survival. Most NGO leaders use their power to dominate the organization and, therefore, fail to be accountable in managing the NGO's affairs.

It is often assumed that effective leaders possess mainly referent and expert power; however, this may not always be the case, as effectiveness depends on the leader's personality, the type of followers, the size of organization and the organization's overall structure.

Many local NGO leaders face challenges in creating adequate time to engage in strategic organizational issues or to build their own individual management capacities. This happens as a result of focusing more on operational issues on a daily basis than on strategic actions.

V. OBSTACLES FACING NGOs LACKING STRATEGIC LEADERSHIP

Better-governed NGOs have fewer management problems and they are able to act on and recover from shocks quickly. This helps achieve faster and more sustainable growth. Unfortunately, the leadership of most local NGOs considers corporate governance and management as relevant only to large companies or international NGOs. An NGO that lacks strategic leaders faces some of the following challenges;

1. WEAK ORGANIZATIONAL CULTURE

An organizational culture contributes to an NGO's effectiveness and performance. Culture determines how the workforce is managed and what tasks are viewed as priority by the leaders in the organization.

In an organization where strategic leadership skills are absent the culture of the organization tends to be weak and as a result the work and team ethics are weakened. This hinders staff from achieving their individual and overall organizational objectives.

Weak leadership creates siloed departmental structures that promote unhealthy competition between teams. This causes many conflicts and communication gaps among the staff and leadership.

An NGO with a weak organizational culture ends up losing credibility and it becomes difficult for the organization to consistently attract and retain high-quality employees.

2. POOR NGO PERFORMANCE

Leadership that is not strategic will have difficulty in systematically identifying the organization's goals and priorities. This leads to goals being frequently changed with no clear vision existing; therefore, the NGO operates more at activity level and does not consistently achieve concrete results.

The organization is unable to consistently perform effectively in its operations and this leads to unsustainable program interventions. The NGO does not proactively take control of defining its envisioned future and it is unfortunately guided by its history and past experiences. The NGO is, therefore, unable to commit resources to those strategies that are critical to achieving its mission and overall performance.

3. LOW ORGANIZATIONAL PROFILE AND VISIBILITY

When an NGO lacks strategic leaders, the image and profile of the NGO becomes distorted among the stakeholders within its area of operation. The leaders are unable to consistently build the profile of the organization; therefore, the NGO is unknown, and its contributions to supporting community institutions or undertaking project interventions are not widely recognized.

4. INEFFECTIVE FOLLOWERSHIP BEHAVIORS

Strategic leadership is critical in ensuring high levels in staff productivity through creating a conducive environment for staff professional growth and performance.

In organizations where leaders lack strategic skills in management low staff morale creeps in, causing low productivity among the workforce due to frustration and intimidation by those in leadership. Employees therefore opt not to actively contribute to new ideas, as management and leadership downplay their contributions. This results to having passive and alienated followers within the organization.

Low employee morale and motivation often leads to a loss of innovativeness which results in the organization losing opportunities that would have improved performance and expansion in the NGO's sphere of influence.

Passive and alienated followers have low commitment to high performance, fail to embrace change and tend to have difficulties in developing effective relationships that are critical to the achievement of the organizational goal. The NGO eventually fails to consistently demonstrate a high level of staff professionalism and institutional commitment that sets it apart from its peers.

A meaningful interaction between the leader and followers is important for developing exemplary followers and creating a high performance NGO. The presence of strategic leadership nurtures dynamic followership attitudes and competencies that lead to increased motivation, team cohesion and feelings of empowerment among the staff.

VI. COMMON PITFALLS TO AVOID IN LEADERSHIP

The following are some common pitfalls that local NGO leadership need to avoid;

    i. Not making time for leader's own individual growth in knowledge and competencies in leadership and management.

   ii. Not making time for individual departmental teams to ensure growth and common purpose.

  iii. Being too hands off or too friendly.

  iv. Not providing feedback to staff on progress, new strategies or information.

   v. Failing to clearly define goals and objectives for the teams.

  vi. Not delegating some responsibilities and decision making.

 vii. Misunderstanding what motivates the staff.

viii. Hurrying to undertake recruitment without having a human resource planning strategy.

  ix. Misunderstanding their roles as leaders and managers.

   x. Avoiding strategic planning and execution and instead focusing only on day-to-day operational issues.

  xi. Selecting the wrong organizational strategy or management style to manage the organization.

STRATEGIC LEADERSHIP MANAGEMENT PRACTICES

It is crucial that NGOs recognize that strategic leadership is a process and not a position. Strategic leaders are change agents who have the ability to focus on both the daily operations and the long-term strategic alignment of the organization with its environment. These are individuals who understand the competitive edge required to position the organization strategically in its sector. These leaders explore emerging strategic opportunities by comparing the NGO's external environment versus the internal organizational scenario.

Strategic leadership requires individuals who have the capacity to clarify the organizational mission, vision, and values; identify relevant organizational strategies, structure, and policies; and create learning processes that help employees develop their mental model to continuously work in an innovative manner.

The following are some key areas that leadership should focus on to build and sustain an organization's performance:

1) STRATEGY FORMULATION AND EXECUTION

The foundational role of strategic leadership consists of determining the NGO's mission and vision. This then assists in identifying, exploiting, and managing core competencies required within the organization.

Most local NGOs envision and desire to reach a certain level of performance, organizational maturity, and sustainability; unfortunately, some have no idea which direction to take because the strategies they have are informal, unstructured, and sporadic.

A strategic planning process assesses the organizational context and helps develop projections that assist an organization predict and respond to changes by clarifying its goals, reshaping its programs, and operational aspects to help it achieve its mission.

Leaders of local NGOs need to recognize their role in planning strategically for growth and high performance within their organizations while at the same time ensuring that the crafted strategies are implemented effectively within the agreed upon timeframe or scope.

Some organizations experience minimal challenges while developing a strategic plan but experience challenges during strategy execution. This is because formulating a consistent strategy is somewhat easy but successfully executing the plan becomes difficult.

Strategy execution is a process that puts plans into actions, and it involves ensuring that agreed upon actions are implemented to accomplish the stated objectives. The foundation for successful strategy execution is having strategic leaders.

When leaders are strategic, they explore ways of creating objectives that continuously tap and maximize the potential of individuals within the organization to improve performance.

The leaders coordinate the identification of appropriate strategic actions and provide guidance on the execution of the plan. Strategy formulation and execution are successful when there is effective leadership within the NGO that ensures that plans are well formulated based on the local conditions and review is done periodically to measure the degree of progress.

In an NGO setup the successful execution of a strategy needs a leader with a strategic vision and competencies that will enable the leader to influence individuals and other stakeholders to perform.

Overall strategy execution practice:

i. is the art of senior management leading the organization to implement actions and decisions that will ensure achievement of strategic goals,
ii. ensures the mobilization and tapping of employees' creativity for the purposes of connecting the organization with the external environment and renewing the organization and its services and
iii. is the active involvement of leadership and employees in undertaking and reviewing actions to find the best ways to make progress.

Strategy execution must be seen as a reflective learning process that helps the leadership and individuals in the organization identify and implement key strategic issues that are locally feasible within the context of operation.

It does not matter how good an NGO strategy is if the organization cannot execute or operationalize it for the benefit and growth of the organization. The leadership of many local NGOs lacks the commitment and ability to progress from developing the strategy to executing it.

Strategic planning and execution becomes meaningful when it is consistently driving NGO growth, performance, or change. Local NGO leaders are now required to oversee not only the successful formulation of strategies but also their successful execution. This is a key role that NGO leaders need to take up while focusing less on the operational issues of project implementation.

2) LEADERSHIP'S ROLE IN LEADING CHANGE

Progress means change, and change is normally stressful for individuals or teams within an organization. Once teams perceive the change as a threat, they create barriers to block the change from occurring, and this can result in a range of challenges.

Change management is an organized approach of moving teams or organizations from one phase of growth to another to fulfill the organization's mandate. It is a process that empowers an organization to renew or adapt to changes that occur within the organization and its external environment.

Strategic leadership means individuals strive to balance the short-term needs of the organizations while guaranteeing a future competitive standing. This requires visionary leadership skills, which emphasize managing the present while investing in the future.

Strategic leaders promote the presence of ethical organizational practices and systematic organizational controls.

Strategic leadership is about knowing how to transfer the changes in the environment to the organization to ensure the organization remains relevant and stable. NGO leadership that is strategic ensures there is a continuous process of aligning an organization to its environment.

They develop a vision that will support the change initiative, and the vision helps to clarify the changes required to assists the NGO take action in the right direction.

Leaders have to build and develop a change management culture within the NGOs they lead for them to perform. Strategic leaders nurture an organization's ability to have a dynamic change management culture through the following;

i. A presence of leadership with distinct capabilities to identify periods when change is required and to manage the process.
ii. Identification and implementation of a set of best practices.
iii. Continual emphasis on strategic focus and support for creativity and learning.
iv. The existence of processes within the organization for managing change.
v. Continuous commitment to the improvement of its core competencies.

Organizational leadership that is empowered, strategic, and motivated will be involved in organizing effective change. Therefore, for leaders to manage change in NGOs, they have to have to have a fundamental set of skills that will enable them to identify, plan, and implement change with the active participation of individuals within and external to the organization.

Resistance to change among individuals or stakeholders is one big challenge that leaders are faced with when introducing change programs. If leaders are not keen to address resistance and other barriers that are likely to affect implementation of changes, then these barriers can slow or stall the change process.

Leaders are required to identify and address barriers to change initiatives at individual, group, and organizational levels. Change management is a required core competency among NGO leaders. NGOs require leaders who are "change agents" with the capacity to communicate the purpose and outcome of changes that are to happen internally and externally.

Local NGO leadership needs to continuously invest in strengthening the potential of the identified change agents and cultivate a shared philosophy of learning that embraces change.

Once leaders support successful change, it leads to innovations that lead to the achievement of the organization's mandate, which is the key to the continued high performance and sustainability of the NGO.

3) PROMOTING ORGANIZATIONAL CULTURE

Strategic leaders strive or seek to promote an effective organizational culture. The strategic leader's role is to define an organization's shared values and image in ways that allow the NGO to be competitive in its defined sector of operation.

Culture within an organization comprises a set of ideologies, symbols, and core values shared throughout the organization. It is good for leaders to understand organizational culture when reviewing and adjusting practices, projects, and programs.

Organizational cultures are promoted by leaders and influence the way business is conducted. Leaders are seen to model and enforce culture through role modeling, coaching, rewards, recruitment practices, promotion, and other ways.

Each organization has built a unique culture that changes over time, and sometimes it needs to change to support a new reality. Therefore, the formation of an effective organizational culture is linked to leadership.

Organizational leadership is a social act, and leaders have a big role in determining and building the culture of choice. Strategic leaders are those who have the capability to explore and understand the displayed or hidden culture that prevails within the organization during various phases of organizational growth that aid or hinder performance.

Strategic leaders recognize when change in culture is needed and make the effort to create an environment that will support that change. This may involve selecting the right people in management positions, assessing individual team performance, using appropriate reward processes, and stressing ethical practices.

TYPES OF ORGANIZATIONAL CULTURE

The prevailing culture that exists can enable or hinder success and performance within an organization. Culture has a great influence on the process, systems, values and strategies an NGO adopts, and this, in turn, has an impact on its performance and viability.

Most local NGOs do not have the capacity and willingness to shape their organizational culture to maximize on their potential. However, high-performance NGOs develop cultures that enable them to consistently achieve success and growth. Some types of culture are:

i. GROUP CULTURE

This type of culture is found in teams and is based on values, attitudes, knowledge, practices, and characters of the individuals within the team. It creates a sense of trust among the members as they develop a common purpose. The focus of this culture is doing things together.

ii. DEVELOPMENT CULTURE

This culture focuses on ensuring that individuals on the team have the skills necessary to achieve their potential. It, therefore, targets the development of individual skills so that individuals become confident and find fulfillment in their jobs thus improving their productivity. A lot of learning and staff development takes place in such an environment.

iii. HIERARCHICAL CULTURE

This is a culture whose foundation is based on systematic and well-defined organizational levels and structures. This culture values standardization and the presence of procedures, and its focus is on efficiency and being stable. Individuals and teams are expected to uphold the policies of the organization, and it is unlikely to drift from their specific job role.

iv. RATIONAL CULTURE

In this culture, objectives are set, and the teams select the most efficient and sensible actions to achieve the goals. They set structures that guide operations and resource allocation, and employees act logically when dealing with tasks and one another.

They quickly adopt technology to improve their technical competencies, and they have specialized tasks to perform. Reputation and success are the most important elements.

v. ADAPTIVE CULTURE

The foundation of this culture is on change management, shared values and behavioral norms. The NGO is responsive and consistently scans its environment to understand the opportunities that exist and then redesigns and designs strategies to capture the opportunities identified.

The team is empowered and willing to take risks, and it thrives on innovativeness for survival. This culture allows the identification of risks and gaps before they occur, and teams develop actions to reduce the impact of the obstacles to enhance the growth or functioning of the organization.

It is a culture that enables teams to view challenges, risks and obstacles as opportunities that the organization can explore to its advantage.

An effective leadership team will support a healthy culture that is consistent with the organizational values, and behaviors that stir up the potential within the individual members toward achieving the organizational goals.

Organizational culture is partly developed and promoted by leaders within the organization. Leaders send signals in diverse ways in different settings, and team members interpret those signals or behaviors to determine what values to uphold.

It is therefore important for leaders to note that what they consistently pay attention to or do not pay attention to or respond to communicates the values, beliefs, behavior, and attitudes they approve or disapprove of. This eventually builds or reinforces the culture in the organization.

Leaders are key and responsible for defining and reinforcing understanding of the deeds and values that promote the envisioned and desired culture within the organization. The health and performance of an organization are often a result of the culture that the leaders embrace within the organization.

Managers and leaders, who are not modeling the desired culture, will have an uphill task to realign the team toward an empowering culture especially if the values and beliefs are not transformed.

The leaders of NGOs are champions and are required to comprehend and oversee culture development in the organization. They are expected to honor subcultures that are aligned with the corporate culture espoused by the organization and penalize those not aligned.

4) LEADERSHIP SUCCESSION PLANNING AND DEVELOPMENT

Many local NGOs often underestimate the challenge of leadership succession planning and grooming. Top leaders often assume they can identify who the promising individuals are, which individuals are willing and have the leadership ability to embrace new challenges, but the reality is to the contrary.

One of the ways to ensure continued good performance and sustainability of an organization is to develop strategies for leadership development and succession. This ongoing process involves a review of organizational competencies and planning for the development of future leaders.

Local NGOs need to define the profile of future senior leaders clearly through leadership development, which means "developing leadership bench strength" and developing a cohort of leaders who are capable of filling future leadership roles.

Organizations need to start developing individuals for specific leadership roles early by evaluating and training internal talent. This effort requires management to understand and identify the expertise and attitudes that potential leaders must possess.

The proactive approach of development and mentorship of new leaders within an NGO is an indicator of a sustainable organization, and donor agencies are increasingly looking for this aspect in organizations they seek to collaborate with.

Leadership succession planning in an organization includes the following aspects:

i. EMERGENCY SUCCESSION PLANNING

A plan is developed for the transition of a senior management leader occurring on short notice. This plan makes it possible for continued smooth operations of crucial executive roles by providing guidance on temporary appointment of an individual within the senior management to assume a leadership position.

ii. STRATEGIC LEADERSHIP DEVELOPMENT

This is a systematic process whereby the organization analyzes and identifies the core leadership capabilities, expertise, and experience needed by the NGO in the next three to five years and creates a plan to develop those capabilities in the current staffing or to hire a new individual with talent from outside the organization.

iii. DEPARTURE-DEFINED TRANSITION PLANNING

Departure-defined transition planning is an approach which the board of directors and management team uses when a senior leader begins thinking about exiting or transitioning from an organization. This plan communicates the transition to stakeholders and involves initiating a review, building internal organizational competencies, and the selection and hiring a new individual to the senior leadership position.

Succession planning is a risk-management approach that is important in building the efficiency and sustainability of any organization. Key strategies of leadership succession planning and development in organizations are:

i. Assessing your organizational objectives and risks.
ii. Using the organizational strategic plan to review and reflect on future leadership needs.
iii. Including leadership development into the strategic plan.
iv. Developing a leadership succession and development policy statement.

    v. Conducting ongoing leadership development.

   vi. Establishing an annual executive and senior leadership review process that assesses performance and potential.

Succession planning provides a clear picture of the leadership gap within an organization, and helps guide strategic thinking.

5) EMBRACE THE DISTRIBUTED LEADERSHIP CONCEPT

Leadership is distributed throughout the organization and in this approach; no single person can make decisions and guide the work especially in a growing or expanding organization. Different members of the organization serve as leaders in relation to specific tasks, needs, and objectives. They depend on one another to achieve larger organizational goals.

NGOs need to nurture potential and existing leaders at all levels by involving them in shaping the strategic direction of the organization. The importance of the distributed leadership approach is as follows:

    i. Helping the CEO to avoid making unsuitable actions or decisions.

   ii. Bringing different levels of strengths, capabilities, and knowledge that provide guidance when the NGO is faced with changing environments and multiple stakeholder relationships.

  iii. Introducing and encouraging the exploration of a variety of perspectives.

In distributed leadership, leaders have the opportunity to learn jointly and have a common view of the future while communicating openly and respecting one another. This enhances the appreciation of knowledge and sensitivity to different cross-cultural issues.

The work of transforming an organization involves improving the leadership's knowledge and the staff attitudes and skills. Using the distributed leadership concept ensures that the NGO leaders are emotionally and mentally prepared to exploit unforeseen opportunities, cope with uncertainty, and achieve tasks with scarce resources.

Strategic leaders are needed at all levels if local NGOs are to adapt, innovate, and succeed well into the future. Hence, the need to view and appreciate distributed leadership as one of an NGO's approaches to developing internal leadership.

6) UNDERSTAND THE LEADER AND FOLLOWER CONCEPT

The organizational workforce is an important asset that needs to be motivated and actively engaged to achieve the organization's purpose.

Followers play an important role in reinforcing or determining the attitudes and competencies displayed by leaders. This is a dynamic and complex situation that many individuals who are leaders in local NGOs do not adequately understand or recognize.

Followership is an interesting concept that is sometimes ignored by leaders in many organizations yet it has a significant impact on an NGO's performance and productivity. A follower's competence, experience, and commitment will influence the leadership role or style adopted.

The degree of relations or interactions between the leader and follower is important for improved performance and growth of the NGO. A leader's high, realistic expectation will result in high performance among followers while low expectations lead to low performance, among followers.

The leader and follower concept is viewed as a cyclic relationship where one influences the other. There is a systematic and interactive relationship between leaders and their followers.

Leadership is perceived as a social process that requires everyone's involvement. The recognition of the influential role of followers and leaders is important to help in understanding the socialization process that models the leadership style an NGO will adopt.

It is important to note that how well followers follow is as important as how well the leaders lead. For example, an employee may approach or view a new task or role with little competence but have a high commitment, or the employee may have high competence but low commitment levels. Hence, the leader's role is to identify the best approach to motivate the individual.

Some organizations lack the right people and, unfortunately, some of the "nice" people who work for organizations are not the right people to get the job done.

NGO leaders need to motivate followers properly for them to be productive in achieving the organization's objectives. Where followership fails, there are minimal accomplishments or what gets done is sometimes not what was intended.

Followership is important to NGO performance and sustained growth. It has been noted that poor work ethics, bad morale, distractions from goals and unsatisfied stakeholders are reflections of followership challenges.

Good followers exhibit the following characteristics: professional competence, good work ethics and judgement, they are courageous, discrete and forthright. Followers need to have the capacity to be followers but also exhibit leadership skills.

Unfortunately, many NGOs that have weak leadership also tend to develop weak followership and the impact is organizational confusion and poor performance. Followers will always be under the shadow of leaders and hence on-going success with weak followers usually proves to be a leader's greatest challenge.

Organizations are said to be only as good as their leaders, and, in addition as good as their followers. Leaders provide an environment in which people can give their best; hence, creativity and innovation emerge.[5]

NGOs need to proactively adopt organizational cultures that build the leader and follower relations and engage strategic leaders who mentor strong followers. This can be done through careful recruitment strategies, constant mentoring, and appraisal of employee performance.

CONCLUSION

Local NGOs are required to be proactive in investing in the potential of their leaders to become change agents who enable the organization achieve sustainable high performance results overtime.

Future NGO leaders will need to consistently assess team performance and focus on strategic issues within an organization to maintain quality and high performance. Strategic leadership involves the following three elements thought, action and influence. These three elements are interdependent:

i. **Thinking**- developing a vision of how or what the NGO should be to remain competitive and increase performance.

ii. **Action**- coordinated tasks or activities are developed and initiated to move the NGO towards its envisioned future. This involves assessing the desired future outcome, flexibility to adapt to new situations and managing identified risks or opportunities. Strategies are then developed that address the desired outcome.

iii. **Influence**- creation of a conducive environment that inspires, promotes synergy and commitment among teams towards the envisioned future. This involves working with internal and external stakeholders to initiate and implement changes that helps the organization remain viable.

Local NGOs that seek to develop strategic leaders within the organization need to look into the quantity of leaders required based on organizational structure, the qualities desired (demographics, diversity, skills), collective leadership competencies and leadership culture.

In some local NGOs, leaders who have leadership traits exist but they cannot consistently achieve the required results, or in some instances there exist those who have the capacity to achieve results but lack the desired leadership attributes. This creates a lot of imbalances and frustrations among the team members and their organizations.

Local NGOs will require leaders who have the desired leadership traits and in addition have the capacity to deliver results that help achieve sustained organization growth. These leaders are change agents who have the competencies and influence to deliver from any position through the use of available resources and information to create strategies that produce results.

An organization's synergy, agility and productivity depend on the leaders' credibility. Credibility determines the leaders' extent of influence and it requires that the leaders' actions and words be aligned to the achievement of the organization's objectives.

Local NGOs that desire to grow into high performance organizations will need leaders who will consistently motivate the spirit, challenge dying strategies, and inspire individuals into action. Therefore, local NGOs require leaders capable of:

i. Envisioning the future and making others see the possibilities in the envisioned future.

ii. Exploring past and present trends in order to foster continuous organization growth in terms of strategy and action.

iii. Focusing on achieving consistent and measurable results through adopting a results-based leadership approach. This approach assists leaders to identify the results needed and enables teams to explore strategies that prompt the NGO to consistently achieve the desired results.

iv. Aligning an organization's objectives to the stakeholders' needs and demands.

v. Building and nurturing their personal leadership competencies. This is known as the self-reinforcing cycle.

vi. Understanding and appreciating the personal or individual values that drive commitment.

vii. Having the capacity to cope and respond to diverse circumstances and manage individuals with different personalities and professional training to develop a high performance multi-disciplinary team.

viii. Elevating the inner voice or human spirit of individuals to increase commitment.

ix. Understanding and appreciating the importance of the management teams and making efforts to harness their skills and strengthen their involvement in the NGO strategic issues.

x. Coordinating the development and execution of the organization's strategic plan.

Leaders of high performance NGOs have the ability to move their organization or teams into action and hold them accountable for achieving the desired results by consistently utilizing information to identify areas for improvement or strengthening.

NGO leaders that are willing to pursue excellence and high performance will need to identify and implement strategic decisions through understanding how their decisions affect the NGO's internal structures and continuously gather feedback from peers and employees about progress toward vision attainment and performance.

Leadership has a huge impact on an NGO's identity and its workforce, and it can determine whether the organization experiences sustained growth and performance or not.

Chapter 2

ORGANIZATIONAL KNOWLEDGE

MANAGEMENT

Knowledge when well managed can assist local NGOs to improve their effectiveness. Unfortunately, many are not able to effectively harness and utilize this asset to improve their organization's performance.

Currently, many local NGOs' systems required for access, storage, transfer, and dissemination of information are underdeveloped. Many face the challenge of having varied and large amounts of data that is difficult to process hence adding no value in enhancing the NGO's performance.

Organization knowledge is an actionable and important component within any NGO that desires to expand its influence or operations within a selected context. Organizational knowledge management can help an NGO to enhance its workforce knowledge base, improve quality of services and build collective action.

An organization's ability to promote knowledge management (KM) practices is becoming increasingly important. Innovative KM strategies have continued to emerge, with a focus on developing organizational structures that enhance the development of new knowledge and utilization of the current knowledge.

Organizational knowledge management is a strategy that supports the use of competencies, innovations, and knowledge to create an effective and sustainable NGO.

There is a positive link between the process of knowledge management and an NGO's performance. When this connection is understood, explored, and planned for it helps an entity be a step ahead of its competitors.

I. DEFINITION AND PRACTICE OF KNOWLEDGE MANAGEMENT

The twenty-first century is an era of knowledge economy and organizations need to utilize information and knowledge that assists them in improving their performance. A critical issue facing many NGOs is how to enhance their organizational capacity to boost performance through harnessing and utilizing knowledge.

Knowledge management is a management approach that deals with the practices employees use to apply and share their knowledge in the work environment.

Knowledge management is becoming an important function for many organizations as they realize that competitiveness lies in effective management of their knowledge resources.[6]

Knowledge management components are interlinked and include people, technology, and processes. Knowledge management ensures an organization systematically creates, distributes, and applies relevant knowledge to make strategic decisions.

KM practices ensure the development of organizational competencies through better use of the organization's internal individual and team knowledge resources.

Local NGOs need to fortify their innovative ability by developing new knowledge as the global and technological environment continues to change if they are to survive and become competitive.

II. KNOWLEDGE TYPES

Organizations use KM processes to identify, create, and distribute knowledge and learning across the organization. It serves to promote a systematic approach to the identification, collection, assessment, retrieval and distribution of an organization's information assets.

Knowledge management is a daunting task in many NGO as most of an organization's crucial knowledge is tacit, and yet organizations are required to identify approaches for managing it for improved performance.

It is, therefore, important for NGOs to understand the types of knowledge in order to exploit them effectively for the good of the organization. The common types of knowledge that help local NGOs respond to emerging issues and situations are tacit and explicit knowledge.

i. EXPLICIT:

It is knowledge that is formal and systematic and can be easily shared. It can be either structured or unstructured and expressed in documents, databases, and other codified forms.

ii. TACIT:

This knowledge exists in individual minds, and it is an "undocumented" understanding about something. Tacit knowledge is received by experience and technical skills within an individual's mind. Tacit knowledge can be further divide into two components;

* *Embodied knowledge* exists in an individual or a group of individuals and may include skills, capabilities, and mental models. This is knowledge that often exits when the employee leaves the NGO because it is within the employee. It can also be described as instinctive knowledge.
* *Embedded knowledge* exists at the organizational level. It was a concept introduced by Mark Granovetter in 1985 and is defined as knowledge that is instituted into a system or designed to ensure knowledge is proactively used. It is found within processes, cultures, laws, values, the organization's strategy, and its codes of conduct.
It is collective knowledge that is found in emergent routines or procedures, and it can be formally or informally instituted in an

organization. This knowledge can exist in obvious sources, but the knowledge in itself is not precise, as sometimes it is challenging to comprehend the benefit of the rule until its actually implemented.

Most knowledge in organizations is at tacit level, and the transfer of this knowledge to explicit is a big challenge. The sharing of tacit knowledge in many local NGOs is weak and many do not recognize tacit knowledge as relevant to the organization's performance and survival.

Management approaches, organizational structures, cultures and leadership styles adopted by the local NGOs tend to hinder the effective transfer of tacit to explicit knowledge in many organizations.

However tacit knowledge is valuable because it is difficult for an NGO's competitors to imitate; hence, it provides an NGO a huge competitive advantage among its peers. Effectively managing this unique resource is what makes some NGOs continue to be consistently innovative and achieve high performance in the marketplace.

NGOs need to understand and evaluate to what extent the existing tacit knowledge is translated into explicit knowledge. They need to explore mechanisms that can be adopted to ensure knowledge sharing is beneficial.

Another serious gap noted in many local NGOs is in the area of institutional memory because most of the knowledge available is stored among the workforce who are the managers, board members, and officers in the organization. Once these individuals exit from the NGO, then the organization loses this tacit knowledge.

Local NGOs have to discover and utilize tacit knowledge within their workforce in order to improve their performance and sustainability. Effective management of tacit knowledge leads to greater creativity and sustained NGO performance.

Few local NGOs have their explicit knowledge adequately stored, and many face the challenge of utilizing this knowledge to improve the organization's practices or make informed decisions for sustained growth.

Explicit and tacit knowledge are complementary and interdependent. Unless tacit knowledge is transformed to explicit knowledge, NGOs cannot share, store or use it. The interplay between explicit and tacit knowledge enables an NGO translate individual knowledge to organizational knowledge to improve its performance and viability.

III. OVERVIEW OF KNOWLEDGE CHARACTERISTICS AND KNOWLEDGE TRANSFER

According to Murray,[7] knowledge transfer occurs when members of an organization pass tacit and explicit knowledge to one another. This happens through discussions with peers, management of organization libraries, professional training, and mentoring programs.

Knowledge transfer (KT) programs prevent knowledge loss by focusing on areas and employees who possess critical knowledge within their minds that is important to the organization. The management of skills and competencies of employees is an important aspect for NGOs to gain sustainable competitive advantage, especially with the current changes in the global economy.

KNOWLEDGE CHARACTERISTICS
Knowledge as an asset has some distinctive characteristics:

a) NON-DEPLETING
Unlike some resources that become scarce once used, the more knowledge is shared, the more it is generated.

b) WIN-WIN SITUATION
Once knowledge is shared with another, the initial person does not lose it.

c) PORTABLE
Knowledge can be divided into manageable units for ease of transfer and management.

d) TRANSFERABLE

Knowledge can pass from one from place to another; for example explicit knowledge can be easily transferred to other people via networks.

e) MOBILE

Knowledge has the capacity to diffuse when people change jobs, technical transmission and during communication.

f) SUBSTITUTABLE

In some situations, telecommunications reduces the need for the physical movement of documents.

It is important for NGOs to tap and share critical knowledge and expertise continuously among employees. However, this is not the practice in many local NGOs, and this can result in challenges when a valued employee retires or changes jobs.

IV. KNOWLEDGE MANAGEMENT PRINCIPLES AND PILLARS

The goal of KM is improving an organization's knowledge assets to ensure accessible and improved knowledge practices. The knowledge management process is undertaken at two levels: the individual and the organizational. The principles that guide KM are as follows:

i. Knowledge is created by human beings, and it originates in people's minds.
ii. Sharing knowledge is embedded in trust.
iii. Technology is a catalyst for new knowledge ways.
iv. The sharing of knowledge must be rewarded and encouraged.
v. Support by management and the availability of resources are essential.
vi. Implementation of knowledge initiatives should start with a trial.

vii. Quantitative and qualitative measurements need to be used for the evaluation of a KM initiative.

viii. Knowledge should be encouraged to develop in creative ways.

ix. The value of knowledge is its use in improving outcomes for external customers or stakeholders. Knowledge is for action.

KNOWLEDGE MANAGEMENT PILLARS

There are four knowledge management pillars:

i. MANAGEMENT AND ORGANIZATION

This involves a commitment to KM initiatives at the leadership and management levels of the organization. The organization nurtures and promotes appropriate behaviors that support the KM programs.

ii. INFRASTRUCTURE

KM requires technology and infrastructure to support its effectiveness. This ensures that available information and communication technology are appropriate. It is important to have KM strategies to manage explicit and tacit knowledge.

iii. PEOPLE AND CULTURE

Individuals within the organization are important facilitators in KM initiatives. Individuals within the workforce have information, and it is important that the culture that exists supports the creation and sharing of this tacit knowledge.

Local NGOs need to recognize that people are an important asset to the organization, as they have experience and expertise that an organization can harness to increase an NGO's competitiveness. Therefore, organizations must engineer innovative ways to capture, share and manage knowledge in an efficient and effective manner.

There is a need for NGOs to manage individuals and cultures within the organization if they are to benefit from knowledge management processes. To ensure support for KM initiatives, there is need to redesign organizational structures and have an enabling organization culture that correlates to sound human resource practices.

iv. CONTENT MANAGEMENT AND SYSTEMS

This includes internal and external procedures that support the creation and administration of digital or paper-based assets. This helps the team analyze stored information to make crucial decisions that help leverage their organizational operations.

V. BENEFITS OF KNOWLEDGE MANAGEMENT PRACTICES

Knowledge management targets the systematic coordination of the knowledge resources available within the organization. The practices of KM are normally done in an informal way in many local NGOs.

The knowledge management situation is unique in every organization because of its unique characteristics. The infrastructure available, the mechanisms the organization develops to capture; and stimulate the generation of knowledge; and the processes of sharing and protecting the knowledge affect how knowledge is managed.

There seems to be a lack of awareness of knowledge management practices among some NGOs in the development sector, and this hinders the sustainable implementation of KM initiatives in the organizations.

It is important for local NGOs to recognize that knowledge is their most valuable asset and the benefits are as follows:

i. It helps drive the organizational strategy.
ii. Ideas are shared across the organization and, this expands opportunities for innovation by allowing ideas to flow throughout the organization.

iii. It helps the organization to be a step ahead of its competitors in the market by enabling an organization to capitalize on opportunities.

iv. It increases employee retention because staff feel recognized for their ideas or knowledge.

v. It reduces costs and improves service provision through improved internal efficiencies.

vi. It builds individual professional skills. This assists employees in undertaking their jobs through effective decision making and problem-solving mechanisms.

vii. It promotes peer-to-peer mentorship.

viii. It facilitates effective networking with other stakeholders.

ix. It builds a systematic organizational memory.

x. There is presence of evidence-based choices that guide the organization in developing strategies for improvement.

The adoption and utilization of knowledge management practices within organizations cannot be left to chance. This calls for NGOs to clearly define individuals' roles in creating and sharing knowledge. This ensures the organization will progressively build its knowledge base.

Organizational knowledge management should focus on building technological, structural, and human aspects within the organization. The human factor is an important aspect in achieving success in KM practices as organizations learn through individuals.

VI. BARRIERS TO UTILIZATION OF KM PRACTICES

Effective knowledge management practices are required to enable an NGO to recognize, produce, obtain, disseminate, and seize knowledge that provides strategic advantage to the organization.

In any organization, people processes and technology will act as either enablers or barriers to effective utilization of knowledge management procedures or processes.

The following are some barriers that hinder effective utilization of KM in local NGOs:

1. INABILITY TO RECOGNIZE OR ARTICULATE KNOWLEDGE

Many NGOs fail to articulate the value of the large amounts of available information and documented experiences that exist.

Organizations that have low "absorptive capacity" do not recognize the value of both internal and external information in assisting to explore and develop innovations. Absorptive capacity is facilitated by research activities that provide organizations with the background knowledge necessary to recognize and exploit information.

2. ORGANIZATION CULTURE

Where an NGO's culture does not embrace learning and sharing, managing knowledge becomes difficult. There will be no use in implementing a process if the drive and commitment to share knowledge is lacking.

Knowledge withholding or lack of sharing is a common practice within local NGOs, as individuals believe that withholding knowledge gives them an upper hand within the organization and that sharing knowledge is not a worthwhile endeavor.

Sometimes the importance of knowledge sharing has not been clearly defined within the organization, and at times conflicts arise on whose knowledge gets shared within the organization.

Organization priorities and resources tend to shift to initiatives or benefits that are quantifiable; hence, knowledge management initiatives are pushed to later phases or timeframes.

Many NGOs view knowledge management as an information technology (IT) function and this creates barriers in effectively managing knowledge.

3. KEEPING UP WITH TECHNOLOGY AND TOOLS

Technologies available for knowledge management have improved significantly, but local NGOs face the challenge of implementing the right technology.

Organizations face the challenge of determining how knowledge should be transferred across the organization using which appropriate tool or technology. Tools and techniques that can facilitate the acquisition, storage, and sharing of information are readily available, but constant changes in organizational structures, workforce and leadership affects the adoption of the required tools.

NGOs sometimes invest in the wrong or inappropriate technology and this eventually causes problems such as cumbersome information access and high equipment costs. This is sometimes evident in local NGOs that receive external funding, and, as a result, tools and technology utilized are aligned to the donor priorities or funding.

4. KEEPING DATA ACCURATE AND RELEVANT

Most local NGOs have old and inadequate knowledge management processes that are informal and undocumented. Ensuring that information is kept current by reorganizing or discarding old ideas is a continuous challenge.

When organizations do not have defined KM processes in place, employees will be required to rely on outdated or inaccurate information. Knowledge management in many local NGOs sometimes focuses on reusing current knowledge rather than generating new knowledge.

A local NGO needs to validate, distribute and utilize valuable data that is generated by its workforce. However, large amounts of data are usually stored or discarded, as they are seen not to add value to the organization.

VII. KNOWLEDGE MANAGEMENT WARNING INDICATORS

Most local NGOs continue to manage knowledge in an ad hoc manner, and few have clearly defined organizational structures in place that support the management of knowledge as a resource.

NGOs are now being pressured to reevaluate the management of their knowledge bases. Some common indicators that would indicate that knowledge management needs to be improved in an organization are as follows:

a) Employees must keep relearning the same things over and over again.
b) No one is certain where to find knowledge that is required to perform a task.

c) It is not clear where the information needed is or who the source person is.

d) It is not clear who has done the task before and what was achieved.

e) The transition of staff causes a knowledge gap because a person has left with some or all the information.

f) There is no documentation of a successful process for the purpose of replication in other projects, units, or initiatives.

g) Mistakes or errors recur within the same unit on the same process.

h) There are huge unexplainable differences in performance among different units within an organization.

VIII. PRACTICES TO ENHANCE KNOWLEDGE MANAGEMENT AND TRANSFER

Knowledge management has strategic implications that are valuable to an organization's long-term goals and performance. Organizations manage knowledge throughout the years, but they do not realize what they are doing.

An interesting fact shared by Kimiz,[8] is that an organization's valuable knowledge walks out the door at the end of the day. This emphasizes the need for NGOs to constantly value and effectively manage its intellectual assets.

It is important that NGOs identify and mobilize their intellectual assets to build its performance and competitive advantage. The four key elements of knowledge management are creating and capturing knowledge, sharing and enhancing it, storing and retrieving and, finally disseminating it.

Knowledge management is beneficial when an organization can identify, generate, acquire, diffuse and capture the benefits of knowledge that will provide a strategic advantage to an entity.[9] The following practices are proposed to strengthen KM practices within local NGOs;

1) DEVELOPING A KNOWLEDGE MANAGEMENT FRAMEWORK

Knowledge goals guide the way knowledge management initiatives are undertaken. Most organizations lose track of their data and information and this leads to uninformed decisions on KM initiatives.

Organizations need to identify key sources, contributors, and consumers of knowledge. Developing the framework enables the NGO to conduct a knowledge gap assessment and create a list of critical knowledge issues required for the organization. A KM framework provides a systematic approach that ensures employees receive support in their knowledge-seeking activities.

The development of a framework also helps to institutionalize KM and learning practices at all levels within the organization. An organization needs to analyze the barriers that will have impact on knowledge creation, distribution, and use within the organization and externally. Once the risks are identified, measures are listed to manage or minimize the risks.

2) BUILDING AND NURTURING A KNOWLEDGE SHARING CULTURE

NGOs can expand knowledge when individuals share amongst each other and new knowledge is created when different knowledge is gathered.

Consistently developing knowledge-sharing strategies or opportunities ensures better organizational performance; however, this must be ingrained in the organizational structures and culture.

The knowledge era calls for renewed focus that encourages ushering in a new appreciation for organizations to attract and retain competent, knowledgeable workers.

Organizational culture is a factor that impacts on the success of knowledge transfer and utilization practices. Where high levels of trust exist within an organization, this tends to facilitate knowledge sharing.

Organizations can develop programs for staff learning that are linked to operational issues, such as how to deliver on development-sector programs. They may also gather content from external networks in forms such as videos that can be used by employees as they work in the various areas of program focus.

Communities of Practice (CoPs) are a good channel for sharing tacit knowledge, as members share and discuss challenges, solutions, best practices, and lessons learned. CoPs are centers of knowledge, where individuals or organizations with similar project responsibilities share knowledge.

Social networking as a part of an organization's knowledge management strategy can quickly develop into a useful channel at a lower cost.

Finally, identification of KM champions is an important aspect in any organization. If knowledge management is regarded as everybody's responsibility it can end up as nobody's responsibility. Identification of knowledge champions within organizations will assist in moving from strategy to culture.

3) DEVELOPING A KNOWLEDGE RETENTION STRATEGY

The strategy focuses on employee development and knowledge retention processes. Organizations need to create opportunities for employees to develop, transfer and retain knowledge through employee development processes and the development of a knowledge profile for critical staff positions.

NGOs need to conduct periodic risk analysis to identify knowledge that will be lost due to retirement, knowledge silos, or the exiting of staff and develop strategies to mitigate the risks. Organizations need to provide opportunities that are developmental and have a high impact on individual and organizational knowledge exchange and transfer.

For example, placing individuals in contexts where they can gain new experience, share learning from a prior experience or move employees across regions and functions within the organization for purposes of building learning capability will enable knowledge transfer and utilization.

4) BUDGETING FOR KNOWLEDGE MANAGEMENT INITIATIVES

Knowledge is a valuable resource that local NGOs can utilize to achieve their objectives. Knowledge creation and utilization is an important management resource and power within organizations where it is effectively harnessed.

Budgeting for KM and learning includes finance, labor, equipment and materials. These are the main factor inputs for institutionalizing and implementing a KM strategy.

Therefore, NGOs must ensure that costs within the budget for KM are realistic. Training programs are one example that an NGO can undertake to enhance its organization's knowledge base. This ensures that individuals within the NGO have relevant knowledge in their areas of expertise.

The amount of resources an NGO allocates to KM determines the extent and level of KM initiatives implemented within the organization.

5) MEASURING KNOWLEDGE CREATION AND SHARING

A powerful way to reproduce and update what works in an organization is by learning from the experiences of individuals or organizations that have undergone or are undergoing similar experiences and hence have ready access to knowledge and solutions.

The objective of knowledge management is to avail knowledge at a personal level and collectively so that effective action can be taken.

Individual-level learning outcomes can shape the organizational culture. However, the measurement of individual knowledge sharing as part of staff performance appraisals is still a weakly developed initiative in most local NGOs.

Developing indicators that measure individual success in knowledge sharing and transfer initiatives is important. This is because the successful adoption of knowledge management practices and learning initiatives is made possible when organizations have employees who are prepared to share their knowledge and generate new knowledge to improve an NGO's competitive advantage.

Knowledge can be developed and transferred through learning and sharing processes. The gains experienced as a result of collective knowledge are greater than individual knowledge so sharing within the organization should be strengthened.

6) CONDUCTING KNOWLEDGE AUDITS

The evaluation and measurement of organizational knowledge is important in the enhancement of knowledge management practices. A knowledge audit measures an organization's knowledge health at micro and macro levels.

A knowledge audit provides evidence of what knowledge exists and its location, knowledge gaps, how knowledge is utilized, and what options exist for enhancement.

An organization needs to understand whether knowledge sharing and transfer occur in the organization, when, and how. It is important also to assess the implementation of the lessons learned to improve the organization's performance.

7) PROVIDING MANAGEMENT SUPPORT

Knowledge management is sometimes political and needs top leadership and management commitment. Clearly, knowledge management has natural enemies and managers play a crucial part in the successful adoption of knowledge management initiatives in their organizations.

Management is held accountable for institutionalization and management of individual and organizational knowledge. Some organizations, with management support have set up information spaces or KM help desks at the office entrance for sharing knowledge within the organizations. It has been observed that to utilize employees' knowledge an organization must have a management culture that seeks to ensure it happens.

This would also involve training and mentoring departmental heads to help them in facilitating staff learning at their various levels.

CONCLUSION

Andrew Carnegie,[10]correctly stated that "the only irreplaceable capital an organization possesses is the knowledge and ability of its people. The productivity of that capital depends on how effectively people share their competence with those who can use it."

Knowledge is what an individual knows at a certain point in time, while learning consists of gathering and redefining what an individual knows. These are the dynamics of the knowledge process.

Systematic and focused knowledge management needs to be a deliberate and planned action within local NGOs, as this helps an organization improve its performance and builds institutional memory.

Effective knowledge management ensures that strategies adopted improve an organization's competitive advantage and build the competency of the workforce. NGOs need to recognize and effectively harness the intellectual capital that exists within their organization for the growth and effectiveness of the organization. Kimiz,[11] states that intellectual assets within an organization are represented by the sum total of what the workforce knows and knows how to do (expertise). For knowledge management to be effective, it has to be linked to what is beneficial and of value to the employees and their professional practice as well as to what will give an NGO competitive advantage.

Chapter 3

STRATEGIC CORPORATE COMMUNICATION

There is a link between effective organizational communication and the achievement of high performance within an organization. Communication is considered as fuel that propels the different functions within the organization, a binding factor that builds relationships and therefore key to the achievement of the organization's overall objective.

Some local NGOs' good efforts go unrecognized because the organizations are unable to communicate their mission, strategies and impact consistently. Many organizations often fail to sell their strengths and capacities in terms of what they have achieved in the past, are achieving, and can achieve.

For a local NGO to attract potential donors or stakeholders and to maintain a good corporate image and reputation it has to build its communication skills and competencies. A good reputation is important for local NGOs, as it influences the effectiveness of their programs, funding, and visibility within its sector of operation.

Local development NGOs face diverse competing priorities such as recruiting and retaining competent staff, seeking resources, addressing communities needs and fulfilling government and donor demands. Therefore, strategically communicating about who they are and what they do is sometimes given less attention, as the focus is more on implementing day to day activities.

However, high-performance organizations invest in developing strategic and appropriate communication programs that support their image, growth and sustainability. It has been observed that high performers are more effective communicators and that highly effective communicators are five times more likely to be high performers than minimally effective communicators.[12]

Organizations need to be strategic in developing communication strategies and practices that facilitate an NGO's influence, competitive advantage and minimizes potential reputational risk.

Strategic corporate communication supports NGOs to proactively explore, understand and interact with key stakeholders to create, maintain and strengthen favorable conditions that support the achievement of the NGO's priorities and goals.

This means that the communication messages and actions developed should be focused and designed to deliver measurable outcomes that support the achievement of the NGO's vision and mandate.

FUNCTIONS OF ORGANIZATIONAL COMMUNICATION

Communication is an integrated process that helps organizations and individuals express and exchange ideas, information, experiences, feelings and thoughts.

Corporate communication is a management function that offers a framework for effective coordination of all internal and external communication with the overall purpose of establishing and maintaining a favorable reputation with stakeholder groups upon which the organization is dependent.[13]

Strategic corporate communication is an approach that supports an NGO's social interactions with its stakeholders and focuses on improving the NGO's visibility and competitive advantage.

Communication is therefore an important strategic and management function that empowers an NGO to influence, motivate, target, generate support and engage with various stakeholders to achieve its strategic objectives. Communication has some critical functions within an organization:

i. Informative function involves providing information to individuals in a team or organization or the process of exchanging information. It involves giving and receiving information that facilitates growth or performance of the organization.

ii. Regulative function involves communication about policies and other regulations that help to maintain the organization. Organizations utilize communication mechanisms to create and share policies and strategies, and this helps in controlling team behaviors through the guidelines and principles documented and shared. It nurtures a positive organizational culture by creating a conducive work environment and ensures compliance.

iii. Integrative function involves coordination of tasks, or work activities and enhances individual and team engagement. It supports alignment of individuals' goals to organizational goals.

iv. Management function involves organization of teams or providing instructions or guidance on roles and responsibilities. It helps managers and leaders perform some basic functions in management, decision-making, and it creates positive momentum for undertaking a project or change initiatives.

v. Persuasive function involves influencing and sustaining individuals or team's motivation towards the achievement of organizational goals or mandates. It assists in altering individual or stakeholder attitudes, prejudices and behavior.

vi. Socialization function involves building social networks and inter-relationships. It fosters a sense of belonging.

IMPORTANCE OF COMMUNICATION

Organizational communication falls into two categories: internal communication (builds internal identity) and external communication (builds external image).The function and importance of communication are often misunderstood or ignored by many local NGOs. However, corporate communication offers the following benefits to an NGO:

I. PROMOTES TEAM AND NGO EFFECTIVENESS

A local NGO has diverse stakeholders who need to know where the organization is located and to understand how it operates. Communication is critical and important as it supports the achievement of an organization's overall strategic objectives.

However, many employees in local NGOs encounter the challenge of not understanding or being aware of the organization's priorities or the organization's strategic focus. Where employees do not clearly understand or receive inadequate information about their roles or responsibilities and the organizational objectives. This causes frustrations, lowers productivity and results in an increase in team conflicts.

Communication helps management present their expectations to the teams and this in-turn helps staff understand how their achievements will contribute to the organization's growth.

Cooperation and coordination among teams are manageable when there are clear and efficient means of communication. However, inadequate communication among teams leads to duplication of efforts and misunderstanding on the key areas of performance.

Communication helps staff have an increased understanding of other departments' focus areas and in identifying areas of collaboration that are in alignment with the overall NGO strategic focus.

Communication helps to increase organizational effectiveness, performance and team productivity. For other stakeholders, communication helps them understand the NGO goals and services.

II. BUILDING AND MAINTAINING RELATIONSHIPS

Many organizational problems emanate from unfulfilling relationships that are the result of inadequate communication between individuals or organizations. An organization is an open system that often interacts with its external environment and receives information that shapes its functions.

Developing strategic relationships with diverse stakeholders needs proactive communication practices within the organization. An individual or an

NGO with effective communication skills or competencies will nurture productive engagements with its internal and external stakeholders.

Communication focuses on relaying crucial information and receiving responses that are critical in maintaining stable relationships that add strategic value to the organization.

Collaboration is not possible without effective communication practices. The essence of an NGO's existence is how it effectively interacts with others as it undertakes its mission.

Efficient and effective exchange of information, ideas and experiences helps to build trust, goodwill and meaningful relationships.

Healthy and meaningful relationships internally and externally enable an NGO to maintain a motivated workforce and high levels of stakeholder commitment.

III. ENHANCES KNOWLEDGE SHARING

When communication channels are open, it leads to increased interdepartmental information sharing, development of new ideas and innovation within an organization. Effective organizational communication builds a systematic commitment to generation and implementation of innovative ideas.

Consistent and effective communication nurtures the development and scaling up of innovations through the feedback received from internal and external stakeholders. Communication provides an environment for the transfer of ideas, experiences and expertise among different stakeholders or team members. When individuals and external stakeholders understand what is crucial to achieving the organizational goal, they will focus on building a knowledge sharing culture and identifying unexplored innovative opportunities.

Effective communication facilitates the transfer of relevant knowledge and strategic information that supports management in the decision-making process. When individuals know their ideas will be required and that leaders will respond to their feedback, they will be open to sharing of ideas, experiences and knowledge.

Effective communication ensures that information sharing takes place in a timely and consistent manner. This promotes synergy and results in increased performance and stable organizational growth.

IV. BUILDING AND PROTECTING AN ORGANIZATION'S REPUTATION

Corporate communication is used for building a strong reputation and improving the overall NGO brand. Corporate communication assists an NGO in explaining or translating its mission, vision, and values in a comprehensive manner.

An NGO's ability to send the correct messages through its behavior and practices is crucial. An NGO's reputation is closely linked to its corporate behavior, and some scholars argue that a good corporate reputation depends on developing consistent ethical behavior.

Staff and leadership of NGOs are active ambassadors of the organizations they work for; therefore, their actions and messages are often a reflection of the organization. When individuals or stakeholders understand and identify with the organization's brand, products, and services they are able to effectively communicate the organization's intentions at various forums.

Individuals are often identified by their words and actions, and the same principle applies to organizations. Therefore, appropriate behavior and messages enable the NGO to consistently secure investment capital, draw the attention of talented employees, and win stakeholder and donor interest. This, in the long run, provides a reservoir of goodwill to draw on when challenges arise.

Goodwill is an important asset that cannot be ignored by NGOs that work with diverse stakeholders. A credible organization communicates to stakeholders that the NGO is stable, a high performer and reliable.

V. HELPING TO AVOID LEGAL LIABILITY

Markets are becoming more competitive, and stakeholders are becoming more demanding; therefore, local NGOs have to keep their communication clear and relevant to avoid legal liability.

Effective communication helps an NGO to understand, consult, dialogue and manage stakeholder expectations and perspectives concerning the organization's mandate and operations in a defined region or sector.

Communication enables an NGO to create awareness on its operational policies, rules and systems to avoid any misunderstandings or negative assumptions. Management ensures the organization communicates effectively in order to align with diverse legal obligations or policies to avoid penalties or malpractice claims.

APPROACHES TO NURTURE STRATEGIC COMMUNICATION CAPACITIES

Despite the recognition of the role of communication within organizations, it is far from being understood or planned for in many local NGOs. According to Paolo[14] the common types of communication found in development NGOs are corporate, internal, advocacy and development communication.

It is important for an organization to understand the functions and purposes of the different communication categories so as to effectively plan and manage its communication strategies.

Local NGOs need to improve their communication capacities and skills so as to effectively engage with a diverse range of stakeholders in order to build their legitimacy, performance and improve their organization's image.

1. DEVELOPING A COMMUNICATION STRATEGY LINKED TO AN NGO'S STRATEGIC PLAN

Successful NGO communication strategies educate, inform, invite involvement, demonstrate mutual respect, persuade and are a hallmark of successful organizations. Managing corporate communication requires a communication strategy that outlines the general reputational position that an organization seeks to develop and maintain with its key stakeholders.[15]

Effective communication is about process and content, and it helps to position an organization's interactions at a strategic level. However most NGO leaders look at communication as just a means to get information to individuals and do not consider the relevance or timing of messages developed and delivered.

Ad hoc and inconsistent communication are a common occurrence in many local NGOs because they have failed to initiate and undertake a systematic strategy to coordinate their communication. NGOs must be proactive to shift from ad-hoc internal and external communication practices to having a plan that helps to improve communication mechanisms within the organization.

Most NGOs lack a functional communication strategy that assists the organization to execute and coordinate communication efforts within its sector of operation.

An NGO should develop a written communication plan that links with the overall organization's strategic plan and that defines what needs to be communicated, the communication roles, channels and governance. The plan should have actionable objectives that facilitate the development and implementation of practical strategies.

Developing an effective communication strategy ensures that all communication is focused on agreed upon organizational priorities, objectives and targeted to the right individuals at an opportune time. It begins with a review of the current communication practices, mapping the audiences and then developing communication objectives that align with the NGO's strategy.

A communication strategy helps to inform employees about the organization's communication practices, and motivates employees to effectively use communication channels established within the organization.

An effective communication strategy increases the visibility of an NGO's operations and helps the NGO exploit emerging possibilities within its region.

2. DEVELOPING COMMUNICATION POLICIES AND PROCEDURES

In every organization, it is important that the NGO creates a conducive environment to facilitate downward, upward and horizontal communication flows. An NGO that lacks a conducive communication environment alienates staff and other stakeholders and this stifles involvement and results in loss of strategic opportunities.

Developing procedures and policies is important as it helps the organization to be more proactive when establishing regular contact with its stakeholders. Policies and procedures are key in building and nurturing an NGO's communication competencies.

Organizations must help individuals to learn to say the right things to the right people in the right channels.[16]Local NGOs need to develop clear policies for organizational communication procedures such as modalities of communication, how big announcements are made, standards for print and electronic communication, approval for organizational messages for public materials and required feedback for internal and external issues.

Developing an efficient communication mechanism requires NGOs to have a clear picture of how communication in the organization occurs and its level of effectiveness. This requires developing a protocol for tracking and reporting progress on communication initiatives developed.

All communication policies and procedures need to be accessible and included in a communication plan or organizational documents. Policies and procedures ensure that communication strategies, tools and practices utilized are appropriate, accurate, timely, and of high quality.

3. BUDGETING FOR COMMUNICATION INITIATIVES

Inadequate funding is the main reason many local NGOs do not engage in effective communication mechanisms. Diverse stakeholders only become aware of an organization's existence and operations by seeing and interacting with messages that define the organization and the services or products that the NGO provides. Communication should not be viewed as a separate activity but should be incorporated into the organization systems and structures.

Local NGOs need to budget for communication processes that help build a strong organizational reputation in the present and the future. Communication methods can be active or passive and it is important that an NGO considers planning and budgeting for appropriate and relevant channels in both the categories to improve communication effectiveness.

It is important that the NGO understands the channels selected to ensure that the mechanisms proposed align to the interaction level desired with each stakeholder and the strategic objective of the NGO.

Resources need to be allocated to key areas in an NGO communication program: communication research; monitoring and feedback; training; development and production of print and broadcast materials, special events and local planning; and stakeholder meetings. Resource allocation for communication initiatives can be done in phases and in alignment to the organizational growth phase, strategy and available resources.

4. LEADERSHIP AND MANAGEMENT COMMITMENT

Leadership and culture are two reasons why local NGOs do not manage communication effectively, both internally and externally. The leadership of any NGO has a strategic role to ensure that communication is managed effectively as it has an impact on an organization's credibility and performance.

Effective leadership involves using communication to influence, inspire and build relationships among diverse stakeholders to facilitate the achievement of the NGO's mission. An organization with strong leadership and management recognizes communication as one of its core mandates.

Leadership needs to facilitate the development of appropriate tools and practices in managing transactional, relational, formal and informal communication. Local NGO leadership should support the institutionalization and implementation of strategies and incentives that facilitate effective communication with key stakeholders.

Leaders are required to recognize and minimize obstacles and barriers that impede meaningful and timely communication within and outside the organization. Leadership and management show commitment by being involved in the development of the NGO's communication plan and ensuring that the plan is integrated into the NGO's strategic plan.

Leaders and managers need to be involved in making sure that the messages shared internally and externally are accurate, consistent and aligned to the NGO's mission and strategic focus.

5. UTILIZING COMMUNICATION IN PROJECT MANAGEMENT

Many local NGOs are involved in implementing projects at the community level. For any project to be perceived as successful, it is judged by the perceptions of project stakeholders.

Many NGO project failures are directly or indirectly caused by inadequate communication among targeted communities and key stakeholders. One out of five projects is unsuccessful due to ineffective communication.[17]

Ineffective dissemination of organizational or project information among relevant stakeholders can result in dissatisfaction, misunderstanding on project requirements and alienation of key stakeholders which eventually leads to decreased project performance.

Communication has become inevitable after the realization that when it's applied at the beginning of an initiative, it plays a crucial role in risk assessment; and facilitates meaningful participation of stakeholders.[18] Communication helps key stakeholders understand the project scope, approach and objectives.

Communication for development is a relatively new social process concept that is not fully understood or systematically applied. It is an approach that seeks a unified understanding, gives an opportunity for interactive dialogue and provides a basis for joint action among all stakeholders participating in a development initiative.

Communication for development helps NGOs to understand the needs, issues, and motivations of all stakeholders who have a stake in the project and to design various communication strategies to win their continued commitment and support.

NGOs should ideally develop a stakeholder communication plan that helps the organization define the key stakeholders, develop messages and appropriate tactics for each stakeholder identified as key to the project's performance and success.

Many local organizations in the development sector are still unconvinced of the importance of effective project communication in development and its impact on project success. However, effective communication has been observed to lead to more successful projects, allowing organizations to become high performers by completing an average of 80 percent of projects on time, on budget and meeting original goals.[19]

6. CONDUCTING PERIODIC COMMUNICATION REVIEWS

It is important that communication both internally and externally is tracked and monitored for its effectiveness. An effective message transforms the intended target audience's knowledge, attitudes, and practices.

Regular follow-ups are required to understand and monitor the effectiveness of messages and communication strategies used by the organization. A communication assessment or review provides an overview and feedback on the effectiveness of an organization's communication mechanisms.

Monitoring communication results involves tracking the impact of the NGO's communication messages on the targeted audience and the reputation of the organization.

An NGO can develop a communication management matrix that will help to capture, review and share the results of communication processes, initiated by the organization.

The review gives a realistic picture of occurrences on the ground and compares with what the leadership assumes is happening. It helps to identify additional communication needs within the organization and this can further the understanding of relevant communication approaches or required upgrades.

Local NGOs need to periodically evaluate their communication mechanisms to aid them stay on the right track and reach their goals. People select brands that reflect their views and values, so it is crucial that local NGOs interact with their stakeholders and targeted communities with honesty and an open mind to get regular feedback.

The same stakeholders and targeted communities can destroy an organization's reputation or credibility just as fast as they can support it. Therefore, periodic communication reviews provide feedback that enables an organization's leadership and management to chart a clear road map to improve its profile and communication practices.

CONCLUSION

Corporate communication is perceived as being strategic when it is consistent and aligns with the NGO's vision, mandate and core-values while at the same time facilitating the NGO's strategic positioning.

Local NGOs are facing a lot of changes both within and external to the organization that threatens their performance, growth and visibility. A strong and credible reputation is an important intangible asset for local NGOs in the development sector.

Effective communication helps an organization to build a strategic position that is unique and different from its "peers". It also helps an NGO build a robust reputation that can be sustained over a long period.

A strong image is more visible and recognized by external stakeholders and this creates a more positive reputation that adds value to the organization's competitive advantage. A strong identity, on the other hand, that is supported by an outstanding capacity to deliver boosts an NGO's operational excellence and sustained performance.

However, it is challenging to maintain a strong image and identity without effective communication practices and competencies.

Local NGOs need to recognize that with the growing social, political and ethical issues that impact on their performance and legitimacy, they need to proactively communicate their desired corporate identity, philosophy, style and structure.

Organizations are required to understand, from a strategic perspective, how they can effectively utilize communication skills and practices to promote the NGO's corporate image and improve the NGO's competitive edge.

An NGO that desires to excel in its performance and increase its visibility has to consistently build its communication capabilities and incorporate appropriate communication practices that reinforce the organizational brand.

Chapter 4

ENTREPRENEURIAL PERSPECTIVES

L ocal NGOs face the challenge of consistently sustaining organizational growth and performance. This is because many fail to re-assess their roles and adapt to their market niches.

Many developing nations have a high number of nonperforming NGOs and many of which face closure. The relationship between entrepreneurial culture and organizational performance has received little attention in the past, especially among nonprofit organizations with fewer than ten staff members.

Most local NGOs become stagnant and are unable to experience growth in terms of the organization's structure, resources or program interventions or services after the initial start-up phase. This is due to a lack of innovation or creativity after the start-up phase and a decreasing ability to recognize and explore opportunities for growth.

Batti,[20] observes that development projects undertaken by NGOs are dynamic and unique in terms of complexity, nature, duration, scope, context, and formality. Therefore, they require the adoption of innovative approaches to manage scarce resources while at the same time achieving expected project outcomes.

Entrepreneurship behavior within an NGO can be described as the appreciation of opportunities and challenges that exist and utilizing available resources to implement innovative strategies that ensure sustained growth.

An NGO with entrepreneurial behavior is proactive, takes calculated risks, is creative, and builds its strategic position among its peers.

Entrepreneurial NGOs are focused on what is new in the market or what is next, or what strategy can best be used to improve the organization's performance or competitive edge. It is all about moving to the next level, staying current and remaining relevant.

An NGO with an entrepreneurial culture views challenges and gaps as opportunities that require innovative solutions. An organization with an entrepreneurial culture develops organizational strategies that keep it a step ahead among its peers and competitors. Therefore, the leadership and workforce attitudes have to shift to redesign strategies that build an innovative organization.

Many local NGOs are developed and initiate projects using a problem-based approach; therefore, mission, and organizational strategies are focused on addressing the current challenges. However, this approach after a while without, the backing of innovativeness may lead to an organization's poor performance and stagnation.

Most local NGOs experience limited growth and competitive advantage due to lack of an entrepreneurial culture. This emphasizes the need for NGOs to start setting up systems that promote innovativeness early so that they become part of the culture within the enterprise.

High performance NGOs are those that appreciate the value of developing an entrepreneurship behavior or culture within the organization for sustaining organizational growth. The opportunity-seeking features of an entrepreneurship culture are a fundamental building block in the survival and growth of an NGO.

Developing nations require entrepreneurial NGOs that are involved in initiating sustainable models of social change in visionary ways. Local NGOs need social entrepreneurs who have ideas and are willing to take risks to lead the organizations into new frontiers.

An entrepreneurial culture enables an NGO to continuously reassess its services and the overall organizational performance. Where a service or operation is not meeting the NGO's objectives or creating value, it is either removed or redesigned.

The lack of entrepreneurial practices or ideas in the early and later phases is a cause of failure and organizational inertia in most local NGOs.

Entrepreneurship and managerial skills are interlinked components necessary for local NGOs to create value and achieve sustained growth.

TYPES OF ENTERPRISES

Entrepreneurs and entrepreneurship are important catalysts for value creation within an NGO that desires to improve its effectiveness and competitive advantage in a defined market. Enterprises fall under different categories as follows:

a) SMALL-BUSINESS ENTERPRISE

This category is composed of those who run their own businesses. They engage family and local employees. The business is funded through their family and close friends.

b) SCALABLE START-UP ENTERPRISE

An entrepreneur initiates an enterprise knowing it could impact the world. He or she explores business models that can be replicated and scaled up for greater profits and expansion of the organization.

c) LARGE-COMPANY ENTERPRISE

These are large organizations that grow through sustaining innovation, offering new services and products.

d) SOCIAL ENTERPRISE

Social enterprises focus on developing products and services that address social gaps. The aim is not to create wealth but to address a social need in a community for the greater good of the affected. This is where most local NGOs fall.

FUNCTIONS OF A SOCIAL ENTREPRENEUR

An entrepreneur is an individual who identifies an opportunity, mobilizes resources, and develops a business to meet and harness the opportunity presented. An entrepreneur manages a business and assumes the risk for the potential of profit.

Entrepreneurs are people who identify opportunities and take the initiative to mobilize resources to develop products and services in line with those opportunities. In summary, the following characteristics are observed among entrepreneurs; they are innovative, opportunistic, proactive, decisive, visionary, and willing to take risks. The functions of a social entrepreneur are summarized as follows:

a) RISK-BEARING FUNCTION

The entrepreneur is responsible for the risks, which may result from changes in client needs or preferences, technologies or new inventions. Risk bearing is an important function of an entrepreneur, as he or she will try to minimize risks through skills and good judgment and will have a business perspective.

b) ORGANIZATIONAL FUNCTION

An entrepreneur is an organizer and brings together different aspects of the organization to ensure it functions well through, continuous management.

c) INNOVATIVE FUNCTION

An entrepreneur creates innovative products, services, and ideas so the enterprise can exploit new markets or opportunities. The entrepreneur recognizes a potential opportunity and exploits it. These are individuals who think "outside the box" and take calculated risks to transform systems or structures for value creation.

d) MANAGERIAL FUNCTION

The entrepreneur is involved in managerial functions such as, determining the enterprise's objectives, formulating plans, analyzing the market, organizing operations, and recruiting employees.

e) DECISION-MAKING FUNCTION

A crucial function of an entrepreneur is making decisions in the different aspects of the enterprise. For example, an entrepreneur will decide which objectives are suitable, which financial resources to secure, and how to manage relations with existing and potential stakeholders.

Local NGOs have to view entrepreneurship as a continuous process and not a state. Many local NGO leaders need to have strong personal and entrepreneurial attributes, technical skills, and managerial competencies to successfully lead their organizations.

CHARACTERISTICS OF AN NGO WITH AN ENTREPRENEURIAL CULTURE

High performing NGOs realize the importance of building an entrepreneurial culture, and they develop organizational management strategies that support innovation and creativity among employees.

An entrepreneurial culture helps to build a sustainable organization with interventions that produce lasting impact and improves an organization's competitive advantage. A local NGO with an entrepreneurial culture may have the following characteristics;

i. They grow and develop at an impressive pace and they avoid getting stuck in one organizational life cycle phase and seek to continuously mature.

ii. They leverage management best practices, borrowing from all sectors what is relevant to the growth of the organization.

iii. They value knowledge and learning highly and take a creative approach to hiring, developing and retaining talented employees.

iv. They have leaders with a strategic focus that ensures the organization leads in the marketplace or is among the preferred partners among stakeholders.

v. They have an expanded collaborative focus that seeks to use a whole system approach in delivering their services.

vi. They are strategically placed or recognized as a change agent in the society.

vii. They continuously seek to develop and initiate innovative solutions for social change.

Many times, NGOs forget to monitor their growth or make efforts to improve their performance once they have started operations. This leads to NGOs shutting down or closing before reaching their potential.

An NGO's lifecycle sometimes resembles that of a plant. This means that local NGOs need to continually receive new and fresh ideas to grow to maturation and produce fruit.

BENEFITS OF AN ENTREPRENEURIAL CULTURE

Due to an increase of NGOs in the development field, stakeholders and donors are always looking for an NGO that has something new to offer that leads to lasting sustainable impact.

An organization also has to show that it has the capacity to grow and adapt to new challenges presented in the development field. An entrepreneurial culture ensures that an NGO does not stagnate or face organizational inertia. Therefore, the benefits of an entrepreneurial culture are as follows:

i. There is wise and better use of limited resources.

ii. The organization pursues opportunities for growth that are aligned to its mission.

iii. The organization nurtures the growth of entrepreneurship spirit among its workforce and reinforces the development of a strong and stable learning culture.

iv. The organization generates new knowledge that provides a continuous stream of innovative ideas.

v. The organization minimizes duplication of its resources and efforts.

vi. The organization develops flexible responses to emerging needs. This ensures stakeholder and customer expectations are consistently met.

vii. It helps to improve the quality of services or products to targeted clients and the demand for services increases.

viii. The organization identifies and seizes opportunities for future partnerships.

ix. The organization exhibits accountability to the communities served through the outcomes achieved.

x. It helps an NGO to integrate growth with innovation and risk taking.

An entrepreneurial culture assists an NGO develop innovative solutions to challenging issues while at the same time ensuring that the organization's structure and operations support the innovative strategies developed. This improves an NGO's effectiveness and eventually its performance.

TYPES OF APPROACHES IN THE DEVELOPMENT OF AN ENTREPRENEURIAL CULTURE

Local NGOs need to embrace an entrepreneurial attitude to undertake sustainable initiatives that improve the organization's overall performance and quality of the programs.

An NGO with a strong entrepreneurial culture grasps opportunities to support the organization's development and sustainability in a competitive market. Most NGOs, as they grow, however tend to lose their capacity for innovativeness or the desire to seek new opportunities to enable them achieve sustained competitiveness.

Complacency has led to many local NGOs stagnating and losing their positions in the marketplace. It is, therefore, critical that an NGO's leadership and employees continuously stir its entrepreneurial spirit, thereby nurturing a culture of entrepreneurship or innovativeness.

a) FOCUSED ENTREPRENEURSHIP

Focused entrepreneurship happens when an NGO has reached a mature stage and does not want to interfere with already established products and services but is interested in venturing into new ideas.

The ability to identify and explore creative ideas has declined and the organization desires renewal. The NGO will therefore, have entrepreneurship as one of the objectives in its strategy. It will identify one champion to spearhead innovative programs, but the entire organization will not necessarily be entrepreneurial. This is a low-risk approach.

b) ORGANIZATION-WIDE ENTREPRENEURSHIP

In this approach, an NGO supports entrepreneurship ideas from its initial phases, and this becomes embedded in its organizational culture. Innovative practices and values drive the behavior and focus of the leaders and workforce because the NGO proactively includes innovation programs in its strategy.

The organization is committed to supporting incremental and radical innovative ideas from its teams. Entrepreneurial contributions are consistently rewarded and failure is considered a learning process.

The NGO takes risks by investing in supporting the implementation of new ideas by setting aside resources and periodically reviewing the organization's ventures to challenge innovative thinking.

STRATEGIES TO CULTIVATE AN ENTREPRENEURIAL CULTURE

Entrepreneurship culture and spirit are concepts that are interconnected and can help build high-performance NGOs. Local NGOs need to create an environment where the entrepreneurial spirit and culture flourishes through all stages of an organization's growth.

Great ventures start with great possibilities and great opportunities and it is important to note that a great concept is not necessarily the best opportunity. An entrepreneurship culture catalyzes organizational change that will promote an NGO's overall performance.

Leadership and management can reduce the failure rates of local NGOs, particularly in the early years by nurturing an entrepreneurship culture that enables an organization to explore, plan and seize opportunities and minimize risks in changing circumstances.

Lack of entrepreneurial practices is seen to be the cause of stagnation, poor performance and failure in local NGOs. It is important for local NGOs to anticipate growth and change early and equip themselves with fundamental practices for management and succession.

It has been noted that continued and consistent performance in local NGOs, is dependent on management that is inclusive and adaptive. Hence, entrepreneurial management is an indispensable factor in the development and growth of organizations.

Due to the absence of the required necessary entrepreneurial management skills and practices, many viable social enterprises with good services fail to maximize their potential.

The following are some practices that can nurture an environment that promotes entrepreneurship at individual and organizational levels in a local NGO:

1) ENCOURAGE SOCIAL INTRAPRENEURS IN NGOs

A social intrapreneur is a person with the ability to see a gap and create a new approach while taking the initiative to act on change. The individual has a goal, creativity, and passion, to see the vision become a reality.

Intrapreneurs are not easy to find and they often come up with unusual ideas that may seem out of context or threaten the normal business process. However if the ideas are exploited further, they can transform an NGO into a high-performance organization.

Local NGOs need to encourage a culture where intrapreneurs thrive and are rewarded. Intrapreneurship enables employees to be entrepreneurs within the organization.

An entrepreneurially managed organization supports employees in developing ideas, exploring, and participating in tasks that might generate creative outcomes. It takes well-developed strategic action, teamwork and communication abilities to implement innovative ideas.

Organizations that value employees' initiatives and talent end up developing products or services that flood the market with great success like the M-pesa(mobile cash transfer) technology in Kenya. Intrapreneurs have the capacity to exploit organizational capabilities to produce goods and services that can lead to successful initiatives.

Social intrapreneurs within a corporate system when identified and empowered can create new strategies or champion innovation within an organization. They act as change agents in companies and learning organizations should encourage intrapreneurship.

Organizations must recognize the need to create appropriate systems for promoting intrapreneurship among employees. Intrapreneurship can assist organizations to effectively utilize employee innovativeness to create new services and products for sustained growth.

2) INCORPORATE INNOVATION IN THE ORGANIZATIONAL STRATEGY AND MISSION

An entrepreneurial culture enables an organization to develop and support the implementation of new ideas. Unfortunately, many local NGOs work with unclear or inadequate guidelines or structures and management rarely rewards creativity or encourages risk taking.

For NGOs to nurture an entrepreneurial culture there is need for a clear connection between strategy, organizational growth, innovation, and operations. Local NGOs need a well-structured, proactive, and systematic strategy to exploit opportunities that exist or emerge at a given time or period.

Local NGOs need to understand that entrepreneurship can be viewed from the individual and organizational levels. The two levels need to be aligned to the NGO's envisioned strategic direction for sustained growth and performance.

Local NGOs need to strategically adjust their program models to seize the stakeholder market demands. They must design, develop and implement innovative organizational processes that will enable the organization to support creativity in its employees, management, and board.

A strategy and mission that promotes innovation ensures that organizational structures and processes stimulate the ability of individuals to constantly learn and seek new ways of improving organizational business. This helps to minimize organizational barriers that hinder the growth of individual competencies and ambitions that support overall organizational growth.

The presence of an entrepreneurial strategy can transform an organization enabling it to consistently achieve its mission and improve organizational and financial performance.

Entrepreneurial perspective helps an NGO to grow and sustain its resources through continuous creativity in service provision, and redesigning the organization's structure. This opens up the local NGO to new possibilities in its operating environment. However, local NGOs in developing nations are missing the opportunity to nurture high performance entities because they lack a strategy that incorporates innovation.

3) VALUE CREATION THROUGH INTELLECTUAL ASSET-BASED MANAGEMENT PRACTICE

A local NGO team with an entrepreneurial culture is alert to the possibilities that exist. The NGO has the capacity to discover and assess an opportunity by minimizing barriers that hinder the creation of a new thing or program.

Local NGOs depend on informal approaches in the management of intellectual assets. The capacity to generate value from intellectual assets is dependent on the management's capabilities and the implementation of relevant organizational strategies.

Intellectual assets are the strengths and attributes of an organization, that are the foundation of its competitive advantage. The key to successful organizational management is harnessing the available intellectual assets and making effective use of them. An organization's intellectual capital includes:

i. HUMAN CAPITAL

This is defined as the capacity of organizational teams and individuals to develop innovative strategies to address stakeholder expectations.

ii. ORGANIZATIONAL CAPITAL

These are categorized customs, culture, principles, and knowledge within the organization.

iii. CUSTOMER CAPITAL

This is measured in terms of the strength of client or stakeholder relationships based on a high value placed on the client and customized solutions that meet the stakeholder expectations.

It is important for an NGO to manage the three types of capital to maximize the organization's capacity to create value. This is why "intellectual asset-based management" approach is important for local NGOs. It ensures maintenance, management, reinforcement and improvement of existing intellectual assets, and it integrates them for application in organizational operations.

Intellectual asset-based management will enable an NGO identify its strengths (intellectual assets) and utilize them to effectively improve performance and sustainability.

The implementation of intellectual asset-based management can lead to a continuous generation of value, leading to an increase in the value of an NGO. It requires leadership to understand the organization's intellectual assets and harness these assets for the good of the organization. It requires the development of an intellectual asset management framework.

4) COLLABORATIVE NETWORK AND LEARNING INITIATIVES

Many local NGOs tend to be internally focused, and collaboration with other organizations is a relatively new practice or is given less emphasis.

Networks are a good learning environment in that network activities help an organization focus on its external orientation. When an NGO maintains consistent and regular contacts with its external environment, this provides additional opportunities and knowledge that can stimulate the generation of innovative ideas.

Local NGOs have to create environments where continuous innovation can thrive in order to improve their effectiveness and sustainability. The business incubator approach also known as "new entrepreneur creation projects," can help NGO entrepreneurs explore diverse perspectives and initiate projects that are feasible and that add value.

5) ENTERPRISE RISK MANAGEMENT (ERM)

Many local NGOs fail to maintain sustained competitiveness in their sector of operation because those in leadership or management have become complacent; there are rigid rules and procedures or a lot of bureaucracy because of the fear of failure.

The objective of ERM is to raise the awareness of risk at all levels within the organization and it supports the organization in making calculated risks as it pursues opportunities that exist.

There is a growing realization that unsystematic approaches to risk management within organizations have not worked and they are no longer acceptable. While some ERM functions act purely as facilitators of a process, others have much more formal powers to develop a risk policy and then to enforce compliance with it.

The challenge facing boards is how to effectively oversee the organization's enterprise-wide risk management in a way that balances managing risks while adding value to the organization. [21]

ERM exists to make risks more open before they affect an organization and it ensures that management decisions are evaluated and challenged before implementation. Risk management involves risk analysis, assessment, and mitigation.

The adoption or implementation of ERM practice within an organization is considered an important determinant of its success. Mehta[22], highlights five broad activities that most ERM programs focus on:

i. Gathering and organizing "risk intelligence."
ii. Cross-functional risk discussions.
iii. Risk scoring and prioritization.
iv. Risk response.
v. Reporting.

It is important that risk- management practices be embedded into an organization's decision making process. However, not many local NGOs have this in place, and ERM still remains a work in progress, or has not been initiated or understood at all.

6) ENTREPRENEURSHIP BEHAVIORS AT THE LEADERSHIP LEVEL

Leaders need to understand and appreciate their role in promoting entrepreneurial attitudes to enable the NGO team to explore diverse strategies that enable the organization become a high performance NGO.

Developing and sustaining an entrepreneurial culture in an NGO requires organizations to be flexible and adaptable but remain viable. Sometimes an NGO identifies a promising opportunity but the leaders fail to allocate adequate resources and sponsorship to support the idea and hence the organization loses the opportunity.

Senior leadership or management teams are responsible for fostering an environment that generates new entrepreneurial skills and project ideas. Leadership has to cultivate behavior that can stimulate an organization to successfully initiate innovative practices by providing motivation and a variety of resources to the team.

Local NGOs require visionary leaders who are change agents and consistently nurture innovation champions. Leadership needs to be committed to assisting the organization's access to resources for innovation and supporting their teams to initiate new project ideas.

The teams are empowered to proactively engage in developing relevant projects within their market environment that gives the NGO a competitive advantage and enables the organization achieve the envisioned organizational strategy.

Leadership has a role to play in the analysis of risks that may occur as a result of exploiting new innovations that may impact on the organization's survival. This helps to build a conducive environment that nurtures an entrepreneurial spirit and competencies among social entrepreneurs within the NGO.

CONCLUSIÓN

Although the importance of having an entrepreneurial culture in an organization has been recognized in the business sector, there is still a striking gap in the adoption of the practice within NGOs in developing nations.

NGOs go through a life cycle, and understanding the different phases of organization growth is important for NGOs to sustain performance throughout the phases. Opportunity identification and evaluation are important tasks for an NGO's survival but they do not come easily to many local organizations.

An entrepreneurial culture enables an NGO develop, strengthen and expand its interventions in alignment with the organization's mission.

The process of initiating a new program or managing a growing organization is integrated within the entrepreneurial process. Entrepreneurship initiatives often lead to changes in operations or products and cause the overall renewal of the NGO.

For an NGO to transform an idea into a successful venture or to support existing ones requires creativity. An NGO can explore the following questions to assess whether the organizational context facilitates the generation of radical and incremental innovative ideas or activities.

1. Does the NGO's management and board consistently explore the type of innovations that would create a competitive advantage in their market niche?

2. Does the NGO's vision and strategy encourage creativity or exploration of innovative areas?

3. Is the innovation proposed an acceptable response to addressing stakeholder and market expectations?

4. Are resources available to promote and sustain promising innovative ideas?

5. Do the existing organizational structures or NGO strategies act as facilitators or barriers to individual or team creativity?

6. Are there any systemic, political, or behavioral barriers within the organization?

7. Is there a sustained commitment from leadership and management to support intrapreneurs?

8. What structures and systems exist to capture, store and disseminate knowledge created by the innovative processes?

9. Are there established mechanisms or scope that guides the NGO's employees to select and explore practical, innovative activities?

10. Are there processes that identify gaps in innovation processes? For example, what hinders the implementation of ideas once they are shared or identified?

11. Are there appropriate, ethical, performance-based and sustainable individual or group based reward systems in place not only for idea generation, but also for implementation that will build unified teams?

12. Can the NGO adequately assess and manage the risks involved in initiating new systems, processes or technology?

To adequately manage innovation and change, local NGOs need an entrepreneurial culture and spirit to enable them be more adaptive and maintain consistent growth. Local NGOs must commit to redesigning their organizations for the purpose of initiating new products or services within the existing operations to improve efficiency and effectiveness.

Chapter 5

ORGANIZATIONAL GOVERNANCE PRACTICES

Once local NGOs expand and become successful, they are faced with the challenge of replacing a single individual or family management approach with a more formalized structure. For example, local NGOs will sometimes face the challenge of replacing a "lifetime" founding member who, although he or she is not adding any value to the organization, still wants to remain on the board.

Once founding members are comfortable having full control of the NGO operations and undertaking tasks their way, it becomes an uphill task to persuade the members to develop an independent management structure or to appreciate the autonomy of management staff that now work for the NGO.

Local NGOs sometimes are faced with a situation where all the board members leave within the same period, which means they exit with a certain amount of skills, knowledge and background with them. This results in a massive gap in the NGO's institutional memory.

In the start-up phase of the organization, board members eagerly volunteer to undertake tasks that are necessary for the organization to grow. The members may voluntarily give funds or resources to implement or support the NGO's operations. Members feel a part of the organization, and they are committed and motivated.

However, as the organization grows and expands, it requires more involvement in administrative work, and the responsibility of reporting on the organization's progress becomes a boring task that is perceived as taking up too much time. Members' commitment and support starts diminishing during this phase.

The roles and functions of the board must change to accommodate its growth and expansion, and this means professional individuals must be recruited to the board and also within the management team.

Sometimes local NGOs face the dilemma of a founding member's reluctance to step aside so that other members can be nurtured to support the growth of the organization. Many NGOs are stuck at this phase because they clearly do not know how to proceed or are too rigid to realize that there is a need to change if the organization is to move forward or grow.

There is now increased pressure from both internal and external stakeholders for NGO boards to become more professional and effective. However, in many local NGOs board management and development are taken for granted and there is minimal emphasis on enhancing board effectiveness. This has resulted in many local NGOs boards ceasing their operations or the demand for their services diminishes over the years.

Organizational governance is the process of overseeing an organization. It involves having overall responsibility for an organization to ensure that its undertakings contribute to the organization's mission and that resources available are used effectively.[23]

Governance is about team leadership that is tasked to ensure that an NGO is managed effectively by providing vision, purpose, and oversight. Governance is a team process; therefore, an individual board member does not oversee the organization. Rather, it is group actions and responsibilities as a whole that grant governing status to the board.

An individual is recruited to serve on an NGO board because that person is expected to make a worthwhile contribution to the growth of the NGO. However, this is not the case in many local NGOs because individuals recruited to the board sometimes add no value to the performance or growth of the NGO operations.

Board members are normally required to serve without pay because they are volunteering and committed to the achievement of the NGO's defined purpose. A board member is perceived to be considerate, enthusiastic, and inspired individual, as well as a change agent.

However, the scenario in most local NGOs is that individuals are recruited as board members, but they have no interest in the growth of the organization. Most members participate on the board for years, without being accountable for the NGO's performance. They fail to understand that they are responsible for the NGO's survival and performance.

THE IMPORTANCE OF A FUNCTIONAL GOVERNING STRUCTURE

An effective board, committed to a purpose and skilled in governance and guided by an effective vision, is perhaps the greatest asset of a not-for- profit organization.[24] There are many reasons for development organizations to have functional boards or governance structures.

1. LEGAL REQUIREMENTS

Organizational operations may be restricted and the presence of a functional board is one of the legal requirements for a registered NGO. Donors and governments believe that trustworthy and ethical organizations are safe places to invest their money; therefore, having functional governance fortifies the legal status of the organization.

2. ORGANIZATIONAL STRATEGIC FOCUS

If the chief executive officer (CEO) is the only one providing leadership, the individual becomes overstretched or strained managing the overall NGO work and handling the finer details of its operations. This makes the CEO lose sight of the wider or strategic NGO issues.

Boards help organizations plan proactively for continued mission success through adopting strategic approaches to enable the organization to respond to the growing demands for organizational services and financial growth.

3. GREATER ACCOUNTABILITY AND TRANSPARENCY

An NGO is at risk of mismanagement and closure if the director alone is the one managing the NGO. The board exists to guide the overall governing of the NGO and for accountability to its stakeholders.

4. GREATER ACCESS TO RESOURCES

NGOs without adequate governing structures often have limited access to resources, since most donor agencies, the private sector, and the government tends to fund organizations that have functional governing structures in place. An NGO with a functional board is able to consistently meet donor and other stakeholder expectations and this increases chances of getting additional resources.

5. BUILDING STABLE ORGANIZATIONAL STRUCTURES

The presence of a functional board reduces and prevents reluctance among the management and staff to introduce management and institutional changes. It helps the NGO reframe its mandate and work through developing and institutionalizing structures and policies that help the organization to enhance accountability, transparency and program impact.

As an NGO becomes willing to change outdated organizational practices, it becomes better equipped to increase the scope and scale of its services. This occurs when there is a functional governance structure.

6. GREATER RETURN ON INVESTMENTS

A board enables an NGO to enhance the return from the investments it makes, which results in increased donor confidence. NGOs become more efficient through streamlining their operations and exploring innovative ways to increase revenues while at the same time meeting the stakeholders' expectations and perspectives.

The board helps the organization map out its programs to identify unprofitable programs that should be altered or removed or others that should be initiated for greater organizational productivity.

7. EXEMPLARY SELF -REGULATION

A functional board allows an NGO to consistently improve its internal systems to give the organization a competitive advantage. Self-regulation gives an NGO flexibility to adapt to regulatory requirements in a rapidly changing development environment. Common regulatory practices include the establishment and enforcement of financial and operational practices, conducting financial or operational reviews, sourcing for stakeholder feedback on the performance of NGO's operations, cooperating with other stakeholders and having dispute resolution mechanisms.

A functional board will also review and monitor the NGO's performance against its organizational peers. Self-regulation helps to build an organization's integrity within its operational area and among other development stakeholders.

THE ROLE OF GOVERNING STRUCTURES OR BOARDS

Many NGOs have the challenge of establishing their boards and nurturing their members, who unfortunately, may not understand their roles.

Board members can greatly contribute to an organization high performance when they understand and are proactively engaged in their roles. The board has the following core functions:

i. PROVIDING STRATEGIC DIRECTION

The board defines the focus of the NGO and is responsible for establishing and carrying the vision of the organization. Boards engage in strategic foresight to pick the best approach to realize the envisioned organizational mandate. This involves strategy setting and development with management and strategic support for management during implementation.

This is achieved through the review and approval of strategic documents and the development of organizational policies and guidelines that continually ensure the organization is aligned to its strategic focus. The board continually monitors the effectiveness of the governance and organizational arrangements to make changes as needed.

ii. PROVIDING MANAGEMENT OVERSIGHT

The board is tasked with the responsibilities of monitoring management performance, implementing projects, approving organizational budgets and business plans, and supervising the purchase and management of major capital expenditures.

They monitor compliance with all applicable government or donor laws and regulations, depending on the context and area of operation.

The board is involved in coordination and ensuring that developed policies and procedures are being adhered to consistently. They oversee the review and update of the policies and procedure documents to establish the required functional decision-making structures.

It is important that the board understand that a policy informs an NGO what to do, and the procedure guides it on the how. Therefore, for each NGO policy developed there should be procedures to back it up.

The board is tasked with the responsibility of coordinating the development of strategic and annual operation plans, to help the NGO develop strategies and programs that are consistent with the NGO's defined mission.

To ensure that local NGOs learn and that programs are enhanced, boards are involved in establishing evaluation policies and coordinating evaluations, and conducting periodic checks to ensure the organization implements the recommendations provided.

iii. STAKEHOLDER PARTICIPATION

Local NGO boards are responsible for developing strategies and policies that support stakeholder engagement in the organization's program activities or strategic goals.

They periodically review their communication strategies to ensure they are engaging with the appropriate stakeholders and sending the right message consistently to external parties to build the NGO's image.

iv. RISK MANAGEMENT

Risk management is should become part of an organization's day to day operations. Boards are tasked with the responsibility of managing risks and ensuring the organization is stable in its operations.

Sustainable NGOs and their boards have realized that ad hoc management of risks is no longer the preferred way of doing business. Board members need to understand their NGO's risk exposure and its financial implications.

Board members are therefore tasked with ensuring that risk assessments are undertaken and risk management strategies or policies are developed.

Board members need to identify the most significant risks the NGO is exposed to and ensure that the organization's management is responding adequately to the identified risks.

v. CONFLICT MANAGEMENT

People within the board and organization come with different perspectives, personalities, and experiences. Some areas of conflict are experienced among board members, between the board and the CEO, among staff members, and between the organization, and its stakeholders.

The board is also involved in reviewing, monitoring, and managing conflicting interests among partners and beneficiaries, especially during program implementation.

Conflicts, if well handled, can bring about lasting change in the organization and if not well managed they can lead to split-ups in the organization. How boards manage the differences will either grow or break the organization.

In addition, boards have the responsibility of managing sources of potential conflict of interest among individual members of the board and management staff. This means board members should be cautious and avoid any self-serving behavior or practices. If an action benefits a board member or director, the action is considered a conflict of interest.

vi. FINANCIAL OVERSIGHT

Board members are responsible for overseeing the financial affairs of the organization to ensure the reliability of the NGO's accounting and financial reporting systems as well as audits. The board financial oversight responsibilities include:

a. supporting development and guaranteeing the organization complies with relevant financial controls and systems,

b. monitoring and reviewing the organization's financial health by paying close attention to the finances of the NGO through periodic updates on the present and envisioned financial position of the NGO,

c. conducting organizational budget reviews and approvals and ensuring the budget supports the strategic focus of the NGO,

d. coordinating independent financial audits and

e. ensuring organizational financial sustainability by making sure the NGO makes prudent investments that bring value to the organization, and has adequate financial reserves at any one given time.

Maintaining fiscal responsibility is an important governance component, and boards should ensure they have a member present who has enough financial competence to ask the right questions to determine the overall financial health of the organization.

Unfortunately, many boards at local NGOs are not effectively implementing their strategic roles due to founder syndrome, inadequate leadership competency, organization size and complexity, ownership, critical external or internal or transitioning events and personal interests of the director or board member.

To ensure continual organizational growth an NGO board has to ensure balance among four opposing elements: organizational effectiveness, organizational efficiency, board performance, and board conformance.

The task of the board is to ensure that these forces are balanced through effective management, strategic leadership, integrated policies, systems, and effective decision-making practices.

COMMON NGO BOARD MODELS

The separation between governance and management is never clear cut in most local NGOs and in some instances overlaps occur. This overlap is influenced by the NGO's maturity, leadership, and size.

Local NGOs in the startup phase may take time to establish more formal governance structures. For example, small sized NGOs with constrained staffing and financial resources may have a governing body which tends to get more engaged in the NGO's daily operations.

Governance models impact greatly on how the NGO operates as they determine how decisions are made, performance is measured and the level of authority assigned in managing the NGO affairs. Some common governance models include:

i. COLLECTIVE MODEL

In this structure the board is composed of a group of like-minded individuals working toward a specific goal. Board and staff (if present) work together on governance, management, and operations, often rotating various responsibilities.

Individual members take responsibility for defining and supporting the philosophy of the NGO. The board members and management staff make joint decisions concerning the governance and operation of the NGO. This structure is applicable when the organization is small and there is a high level of agreement and commitment to the value of the NGO.

ii. ADVISORY BOARD MODEL

This model emphasizes the supportive role of the board and occurs where the director is the founder of the NGO. Board members are occasionally required to give advice and endorse the NGO director's recommendations.

The board members are recruited by the founder who is also the director and sometimes the members end up being controlled by the director. This board may be perceived as providing legitimacy to the organization but it governs in a theoretical sense.

Board meetings are guided by the agenda developed by the director with little input from other members and the meetings tend to be informal and task-oriented.

iii. ADMINISTRATIVE OR OPERATIONAL MODEL

In the administrative or operational model, board members undertake the governance, management, and operational functions of the NGO. Board members are tasked with the direct implementation and administration of the organization.

If resources are available, the staffing structure tends to be quite informal. The organization may have a minimal number of staff who volunteer or work part-time and are sometimes paid an allowance. This structure is applicable when the organization is small in either membership or available resources.

iv. POLICY GOVERNANCE MODEL

When an NGO expands and there is growth and an increase in staff and organizational operations the policy governance model becomes appropriate structure to adopt.

The board's focus is on the vision, mission, values, and strategic priorities of the organization. Therefore, it leads by articulating and developing policies to assist the NGO in developing organizational aims, governance structures, and management boundaries.

The policies stipulate the interactions between the director and members of the board and this board rarely works through committees. The board is tasked with the role of hiring and supervising the director of the organization.

v. TRADITIONAL MODEL

In this model, the board members develop committees that oversee the governance and management operations of the NGO. These committees are formed based on functional lines for example, programs or resource development while the management role is the responsibility of the director.

vi. RESULTS-BASED MODEL

In the results-based model the NGO director is a nonvoting member but has major influence over decisions or processes within the board. This is an emerging governance model whereby committees are constituted around board functions.

The board members are involved in planning, guiding the leadership of the NGO, and monitoring and reviewing board performance, the director, and the overall NGO operations.

Every local NGO has its own culture based on a specific set of variables. Determining an appropriate governance model requires more than choosing an approach from a list of possible options. It involves an individual's understanding and appreciation of how diverse aspects of governance will influence an organization's operations.

Therefore, each NGO should select a model that suits its context and the size of the organization so as to support the organization to consistently achieve its mission.

Once an NGO has selected its governance structure, it is helpful and recommended for the board team to seek training to help them understand the model selected and the roles of the board in the selected model. Refresher training is an important ongoing practice for the existing board members and also to orient the incoming members.

BOARD COMPOSITION

The board's composition has to be managed to ensure there are individuals with the appropriate and relevant expertise and experience. The board needs to create diversity and ownership to sustain its effectiveness.

Local NGO boards have to recruit individuals with the appropriate competencies, expertise, values and perspective. Inclusiveness is achieved when a board strategically ensures it has a balanced proportion of members in terms of gender, age, and ethnicities, relevant stakeholders and representatives of the communities being served.

When boards are well structured and clear systems are established on board coordination, they tend to maximize the expertise of individual members and achieve the mission of the NGO.

Balanced member involvement is important for enriching discussions and inclusive decision-making. Effective boards are those that develop and maintain high levels of involvement, at both the overall board and committee levels.

The size and context of an NGO will determine the number of board members an organization can have. The ideal average for small to medium NGOs is to have five to nine members. However an NGO should choose a board size that will enable it to:

i.   manage productive and constructive meetings,
ii. build the organization's reputation and profile,
iii. make quick and appropriate decisions,
iv. ensure that the board can efficiently coordinate and organize the tasks and activities of its committees, and
v.   monitor and review the organization's performance and ensure the NGO operates effectively.

SELECTION AND RECRUITMENT OF BOARD MEMBERS

Effective recruitment of members is an energy and time consuming activity. However, it needs to be viewed as an ongoing activity in the life of the organization. Many NGOs tend not to be aggressive or proactive in the recruitment of board members and this leads to failure and stagnation in many organizations.

Recruiting, developing, and retaining appropriate individuals to serve in a board is a difficult and time-consuming job. However, healthy organizations are willing to make a major investment of time and effort in these activities to build a strong board.[25]

During the recruitment of potential board members, it is essential to consider their technical expertise and their personal traits. For example, it would be inappropriate to select an individual who has an impressive professional experience yet does not embrace a team approach.

LEADERSHIP ATTRIBUTES REQUIRED IN BOARD MEMBERS

Board composition is important for enhancing the linkages, between an NGO's strategic position and its image.

MacDonald,[26] cautions that board members' actions and their relationship to the community can influence the success of an organization. Therefore, recruitment of the board members requires a strategic approach to get the appropriate individuals.

Individuals may volunteer to serve on a board for diverse reasons. Some reasons for an individual to volunteer on a local NGO board include;

i. The desire to build the member's and the NGO's principles.
ii. Increasing knowledge about a development issue or cause.
iii. One way of giving back to the community.
iv. Getting an opportunity to use his/or her expertise and experience and find personal fulfillment.

If an individual has the above perspective, it makes involvement in a board fulfilling. It is however important that there is alignment between the individual's motivation to participate in the board and the NGO's purpose of recruiting the individual members.

Local NGOs need to identify and recruit board members who are visionary, adaptable, independent thinkers, mission oriented, inspirational, creative, and team players. The following are some attributes required among board members:

i. THE INTELLECTUAL DIMENSION

This dimension entails the capacity for critical analysis and judgment, vision and imagination, strategic perspective, and decision-making

The individual maintains independence of thought in critically analyzing the NGO's options and is willing to invest in the organization by developing strategies and being proactive in supporting the NGO's goals. The individual has a future orientation that desires to see the organization progress from the present state to desired state that ensures the NGO remains effective.

ii. THE MANAGERIAL DIMENSION

The managerial dimension entails having resource-managing skills, being a good communicator, having the ability to motivate and empower others, being results focused and having a high level of commitment.

This person has a willingness and ability to carry out his or her responsibilities and develop and maintain healthy relationships with major stakeholders. The individual has a broad perspective on issues and is willing to question, explore, and consider different opinions.

iii. THE EMOTIONAL AND SOCIAL DIMENSION

This dimension entails having an individual who is self-conscious, insightful, interpersonal, persuasive, and meticulous and who has emotional strength and cultural sensitivity.

This enables the individual to manage the team dynamics and effectively take action that is aligned to the NGO's political situation.

INDIVIDUAL BOARD MEMBER ROLES

Overburdening the most passionate board members will probably reduce their future involvement on the board. The pitfall many NGOs enter into occurs when a board member exits and they fail to recruit a replacement. After a while, the board has fewer members and they eventually experience burnout.

Board members will undertake their roles effectively if there is clarity about their roles and jurisdictions. Each individual on the board has a crucial role in the governance of the NGO. These roles include:

i. providing direction and guidance to the NGO's management team,
ii. attending board meetings and actively participating in discussions,
iii. supporting decision making,
iv. being actively involved in board level committees,
v. consistently being aware of the issues that the NGO seeks to undertake,
vi. understanding the organization's current operations through conducting visits to project sites, attending meetings with staff, or reading organizational reports,
vii. representing the interests of the organization among external stakeholders where appropriate and
viii. monitoring and reviewing the board and NGO performance periodically.

It is important that each board member gets a copy of the board charter which has all the crucial information about the board's operations and functions. However, this manual has to be periodically reviewed to reflect the board's and the NGO's internal and external changing environments.

Boards need to consider using staggered appointment terms for the members to avoid having a leadership vacancy within the board. For example, some board executives can have a three-year term while the other members can be allocated a two-year term. This will help to ensure members will not all exit at the same time when their board terms end.

It has been observed that having an odd number of board members will keep the system of checks and balances in good working order.

TYPES OF BOARD COMMITTEES

Ideally, boards should establish board-level committees to help the board conduct its business because it may be difficult or impractical for the full board membership to be present or engaged consistently to effectively fulfill its expectations.

The establishment or the number of committees an organization may have at a given point is determined by individual NGO contexts. Regardless of how many committees an NGO establishes, it should always be clear that the full board has the final oversight of the NGO's operations.

The aim of setting up committees is for them to undertake certain areas of responsibility in greater detail and then provide feedback to the full board on the committee's work as well as recommendations for board actions.

There are two categories of committees within an NGO's board:

a) STANDING COMMITTEES

Standing committees are permanent or operational committees and they are documented in the NGO's bylaws.

b) AD HOC COMMITTEES

These are temporary committees established for a particular purpose and are disbanded once the task is accomplished. For example, as an NGO expands and there is a need for more office space.

A team is tasked to look at the best options to expand the existing NGO office. This team oversees the opening up of new offices and is disbanded once the task is completed.

The following are some examples of board committees that an NGO may have that fall under the two categories:

1. BOARD DEVELOPMENT COMMITTEE

This committee's functional role is to provide support when the NGO needs to identify new board members and develop the overall board to enhance its effectiveness.

For example, if the board needs to recruit a new member, this team will search for potential members and choose appropriate individuals to recruit. It then assigns a recruiter or a nomination committee to approach each individual. In addition, this team has the responsibility of inducting new members and monitoring and reviewing the board's effectiveness.

2. FINANCE COMMITTEE

This committee reviews and monitors the organization's financial position and offers recommendations to the board on budgeting and financial aspects.

3. RESOURCE DEVELOPMENT COMMITTEE

This committee is responsible for overseeing fundraising and other activities designed to ensure adequate financial resources for the organization.

4. PROGRAM COMMITTEE

The members prepare recommendations relating to the direction of each program, monitor program activities and results, and oversee program planning.

5. PUBLIC RELATIONS COMMITTEE

Members are responsible for the overseeing aspects of public accountability, including promotional materials, communications with the public and press, representing the organization in the community, responding to inquiries, and disaster communications.

6. EXECUTIVE COMMITTEE

As the NGO grows, it becomes necessary to call unplanned meetings to discuss emerging issues. However, it is difficult to have full representation during unplanned meetings due to the geographic distances or personal schedules.

To avoid stalling the decision making processes that are crucial to the NGO's operations this committee is selected to act on behalf of the overall board. This team is important in handling decisions that need to be made quickly or within a short duration.

7. SUB-COMMITTEES

A subcommittee has specific tasks and reports to a standing committee within the board. For example, a nominating sub-committee will report to the Board Development Committee.

REASONS FOR HAVING BOARD COMMITTEES

Splitting the board into committees helps:

   i. the overall board team accomplish the NGO's mission and purpose,
  ii. improves the board's effectiveness in undertaking their roles and responsibilities,
 iii. assists the board in making informed strategic decisions,
 iv. harness the individual board members' skills and expertise and
  v. provides more opportunities for individual members to meaningfully participate.

The primary role of committees is advisory with final decisions being the responsibility of the full board. Each standing committee should be identified in the organization's bylaws and should align with the NGO's mandate. This is an area where most local NGOs have a challenge.

CHALLENGES FACING LOCAL NGO BOARDS

NGO boards face diverse challenges that affect their growth and effective management as follows:

i. Individual board members are unwilling or have inadequate expertise to undertake their responsibilities.

ii. The board over relies on the initial vision of some of the original board members. The team therefore faces the challenge of not moving to a common understanding as the NGO expands. The board does not go out of its way to learn about innovations tried by others and ends up lacking in new ideas and perspectives.

iii. Boards focus on the operational or day-to-day operations of the NGO; hence, they are unable to operate at a strategic level.

iv. Many individual members are unmotivated or not committed to the mission of the organization and its growth. Therefore, minimal attention is given to program results or organization growth. This often leads to conflicts between the board and management.

v. The boards do not periodically assess their own performance. They have difficulties reflecting and reviewing their governance practices.

vi. Most NGO board compositions and structures are inadequate or underdeveloped. Two reasons for this are that NGOs face difficulties in getting committed and willing individuals to volunteer and ongoing board development is not planned for.

vii. Board chairs and members have challenges with the dynamics of managing diverse personalities and developing the team. This creates mistrust and frustration, as members are not comfortable expressing their opinions or ideas.

viii. Members avoid accountability, as they hesitate to hold one another accountable for ensuring the organization and board adhere to the decisions or performance standards set, or they are not given opportunity to hold one another accountable.

ix. The board members have minimal or no engagement in resource mobilization initiatives. Many are not clear on their roles in fundraising for the organization and some lack the necessary skills.

x. Some board members face conflict of interest challenges as they have unchecked individual authority over the management of staff.

xi. Many NGO boards lack a board vision, comprehensive bylaws, policies, or charters to guide the overall management of the board.

OVERVIEW OF BOARD DEVELOPMENT COMPONENTS

Establishing and building up the board is an essential task in maintaining a stable governance foundation for an NGO. The board development components can help an NGO leadership address some of the challenges they face in the establishment and development of an effective board structure.

Sustainable NGOs provide and support annual and ongoing investment in developing existing and new leaders within the organization at management and board levels. The key components in board development are:

i. RECRUITMENT AND APPOINTMENT

Organizations are dynamic; they grow and change with emerging community needs. Therefore, a criterion that stipulates the process of recruitment and selection of new members is important. [27]

As the organization matures it may decide to embark on a new programmatic area of focus. Then it will need to add members with technical expertise in that area to successfully steer the organization to achieve its focus.

The selection criterion needs to be reviewed periodically to capture emerging issues in the board's dynamics. It is a good practice for an NGO to design a profile that indicates the skills, experiences, and attitudes that an organization is looking for in its potential members.

Member recruitment is a critical task in developing the board size and composition. There is a need to identify a wide range of options to source for potential members and it is important to have a board recruitment plan.

ii. ORIENTATION

Orientation involves familiarizing new members on their roles and responsibilities, and the organization mission's and guiding documents. It involves providing each individual with an orientation packet that includes information about the NGO's purpose, existing and upcoming projects and funding sources, a schedule of meetings, board job descriptions, committee member assignments, tenure in office and financial support expectations; an inventory of existing board members and staff, the board charter, and a recent NGO report.

The NGO can plan for one to two day meetings for orientation and may consider involving an external consultant to assist the team in undertaking the exercise, to build the team's competence.

One tool that boards can adopt to achieve their strategic roles is a board portal that gives updates on current overall NGO documents articles, and board reports. This mechanism provides space for interactions through questions and comments.

iii. TRAINING

Board engagement done in an ad hoc manner or at annual presentations of the NGO's progress has proved to be ineffective. The purpose is to build new competencies and provide additional knowledge among existing board members.

The training should focus on leadership and personal competency building courses. Boards need to learn from others through identifying similar or like-minded organizations they perceive to have effective boards, learning from their experiences and selecting relevant practices to adopt.

Ensuring that board members are continuously engaged and learning will improve board effectiveness and innovativeness.

iv. EVALUATION

Evaluation is an annual activity to evaluate the individual members' contributions to the board and the organization. In addition the board gets an opportunity to evaluate its performance and to plan for improvements as a team. For boards to grow and develop it is necessary to invest in board-member development and develop a culture of continuous learning.

Periodic performance review of the board and its members helps the board perform efficiently. The board can use tools such as board progression matrix and an annual action plan to help evaluate its effectiveness and efficiency.

v. RECOGNITION OF COMMITMENT

Recognition is the process of appreciating and recognizing achievements of the board and NGO objectives. Recognition shows that the board values its member's commitment and contribution to the success of the organization.

The development elements discussed above are critical to the success of the NGO; therefore, it is prudent to establish a functional board development committee whose main task is to oversee activities that ensure the board's growth. This committee can also seek the services of an external consultant for additional support and accountability.

CONCLUSION

Boards are ideally responsible for determining the purpose of the organization, its continuity, progress and identity. Governance is about overseeing and ensuring, rather than doing.[28] It means ensuring that the NGO is well managed, without having to be involved in the management.

NGOs are dynamic and they advance and evolve during different organizational phases. In each phase, the NGO has distinctive requirements or traits that may necessitate board participation or engagement or a different form of governance structure. For example, a local NGO that is just starting out will need board members with competencies in developing bylaws, designing programs and experience in mobilizing funding.

A functional NGO board ensures the NGO develops stable internal control processes that will provide a realistic assurance of the attainment of the NGO's purposes in the following areas:

    i.   The quality and effectiveness of the NGO's processes.
    ii. Consistency in financial management and reporting.
   iii. Conformity and alignment to applicable laws and regulations within the region of operation.

Changes may also be required within the board as the organization expands or modifies its operations. This requires boards to periodically relook at the NGO's existing and future operations so as to align board functions and roles to support the achievement of the NGO's envisioned mandate and avert possible risks in addition to focusing on operations.

Board members need to remember that they cannot profit from their service to the organization, and, in a small NGO that is still in its growing phase the board may be required to participate in the NGO's daily operations. But this involvement should gradually phase out as the organization expands.

Creating the right board culture increases the commitment and value of board members to the organization. The board must comprehensively review its role and committee tasks so that they are well structured to increase team synergy.

There is no single approach to governance that is suitable for every organization. Each NGO board should select and use practices from governance models that best suit their context while maintaining perspective on organizational strategic priorities and risks.

Chapter 6

ORGANIZATIONAL SUSTAINABILITY PRACTICES

Sustainability is important for any local NGO's future success and competitive edge in the current and future development focus. Many NGOs are searching for creative strategies to support the establishment of a viable entity that ensures achievement of organizational mandate through realization of positive outcomes at community level.

However, many local NGOs are struggling to maintain a high level of performance and to expand consistently once the NGO is initiated and as a result many end up closing down after a brief period of being in existence. Others become stagnant once external funding ends.

Organizational sustainability is the least prioritized or planned for aspect in many local NGOs. Many are not actively managing the sustainability of their organizations and this eventually leads to reduced performance over time.

Sustainability is the ability of an NGO to fulfill its organizational purpose and address the needs of its stakeholders over time. It can also be defined as the ability of an NGO to strengthen its internal capabilities to enable it to expand and adopt management practices that enable it to consistently achieve its purpose.

Sustainability is a process that entails making strategic decisions that enhance the functionality of an organization to consistently achieve its mandate at a given period of time. It is therefore becoming necessary for local NGOs to embrace management practices that enhance organizational effectiveness and sustainability.

Organizational sustainability is a complex and dynamic process that is often influenced by changes in the internal and external environment. Sometimes an NGO's focus is primarily on one aspect of sustainability, yet it is crucial to explore other sustainability factors or perspectives that impact on the NGO's growth and performance.

There is now a growing realization that local NGOs are required to identify and nurture internal sustainability management aspects to improve performance and viability.

Many views are shared on organizational sustainability. Some scholars argue that an NGO's sustainability is influenced more by culture and leadership than by specific procedures. Others argue that organizational sustainability is about taking a long-term view and developing meaningful strategies that shape an organization to remain relevant in the market or its niche.

However organizational sustainability should not be viewed as a one off event or activity and it cannot be achieved by undertaking short-term initiatives. Organizational sustainability is a journey or a direction of travel and should be seen as a process that requires continuous creation of systematic processes and structures to build a viable NGO.

Organizational sustainability requires NGOs to examine the internal and external surroundings in which they operate in. This helps to identify whether the NGO provides a conducive environment for sustainable programs or steady organizational growth.

There are three types of sustainability that can be used to understand elements of internal sustainability among local NGOs:

i. FINANCIAL SUSTAINABILITY

Financial sustainability is measured by an organization's net income, liquidity, and solvency. It is the capacity to secure and manage resources adequately to ensure the organization meets its planned objectives. This means the organization builds on its self-reliance through diversification of income and accessing diverse resources to enable the organization to achieve its mission. In addition, the organization has strong grantsmanship and financial management competencies.

ii. INSTITUTIONAL SUSTAINABILITY

A sustainable organization has a mission and a vision that provides a road map for the NGO. Institutional sustainability means the organization has robust and innovative management practices that govern the organization to help it achieve its mandates consistently over time.

The NGO has a strategic focus that guides the implementation of its mission, and this is reviewed to ensure that the organization is on track. A sustainable organization strategically aligns its mission and organizational systems to adapt to the prevailing internal and external situation so that it can remain relevant.

The leadership within the organization is responsible for supporting and guiding the organization to implement strategies that effectively lead to the maturation and expansion of the NGO.

iii. PROGRAMMATIC SUSTAINABILITY

The organization provides or engages in project interventions that transform the communities being targeted and continue long after external funding has ended. The organization has a strategic and defined purpose to select and intervene in activities or projects it can sustain over time. This is sometimes referred to as the sustainability of services.

The three sustainability elements are interdependent and interlinked and therefore a balance has to be maintained among the three components, as a change in one will result in a change in the others. Many individuals assume that an NGO's sustainability is based on its financial strength; however; financial stability alone becomes immaterial and pointless over time.

THE IMPORTANCE OF INTERNAL SUSTAINABILITY INITIATIVES

For an NGO to be successful in achieving sustainability it needs a vision and strategy to support sustainability initiatives within the organization.

There must be full commitment toward the process within the organization because sustainability is a process that needs to be continually managed and monitored.

Proactively adopting sustainability initiatives among NGOs has the following benefits:

i. It builds the NGO's capacity to undertake the envisioned mission in a targeted community over an extended period of time.

ii. It ensures the NGO achieves greater impact because products and services are of high quality and consistently meet stakeholder needs.

iii. It provides the organization with the capacity to influence certain aspects in the external environment to its advantage.

iv. It reduces risks and enables the NGO to deal with uncertainties. It reduces the impacts of external threats that may affect an NGO's survival.

v. It helps the NGO develop a diversified funding or resource base.

vi. It builds an NGO's reputation among its peers and other stakeholders and hence enables the NGO secure resources through attracting and retaining donors.

vii. It enables an NGO to identify new opportunities for growth.

viii. It attracts and retains a competent and productive workforce.

ix. It improves an NGO's viability which contributes to a stronger civic society in the region or sector the NGO operates in.

x. It supports in the development of sound internal management systems that enable the organization to be responsive to its changing environment.

xi. It helps an organization build a culture of continuous internal learning by identifying and addressing existing critical performance gaps.

Unfortunately, the incorporation of sustainability initiatives or practices is the least prioritized or planned for component in many local NGOs. The leadership and management of most NGOs are not actively managing the sustainability of their organizations, and this can be attributed to a limited understanding of what it entails to have a sustainable NGO or giving more focus on one aspect of organizational sustainability mostly the financial aspect. This eventually leads to reduced performance over time.

FOCUS ON ORGANIZATIONAL INTERNAL SUSTAINABILITY PRACTICES

Sustainability is an aspect that any NGO that desires to grow needs to focus on. Sustainability relates to an NGO's ability to sustain its mission and ongoing operations over time.

The process of sustainability is complex and continuous, and it is worthwhile to note that some organizations are more likely to be sustainable than others. Several factors are observed from the author's field experiences and literature by other development practitioners that are helpful in enhancing an organization's sustainability efforts.

These in turn will influence an organization's ability to maintain a competitive edge among its peers.

Local NGOs need to adopt diverse institutional management practices that will enhance organizational sustainability and eventually lead to high performance. These practices fall under the three sustainability categories discussed;

a) INSTITUTIONAL SUSTAINABILITY

1. Organizational structure.
2. Organizational culture.
3. Organizational strategy.
4. Governance.
5. Change management.
6. Human resource management.

b) PROGRAMMATIC SUSTAINABILITY

7. Program delivery.
8. Maintaining partnerships.
9. Organizational learning.

c) FINANCIAL SUSTAINABILITY

10. Resource development.
11. Financial governance.

The above aspects are interlinked and interdependent and may also cut across the categories. Local NGOs may need to strengthen the following institutional management practices to increase the likelihood of building a viable organization and managing the overall performance of the NGO.

1. DEVELOPING A FLEXIBLE AND RESPONSIVE ORGANIZATIONAL STRUCTURE

A structure is a valuable management tool that helps in the coordination and division of teams to achieve organizational goals. A high performance NGO requires a structure that maximizes its efficiency and sustainability based on its context, size, operations, and ownership.

Increased competition in the development field requires local NGOs to think strategically about appropriate organizational structures that will support the accomplishment of the NGO's goals with efficient use of resources. This is because a structure articulates the organizational focus or mandate.

Local NGOs that were in the past shielded from competition are now required to embrace new knowledge, technology, standards and attitudes for optimal performance. For example, a structure that allows for a decentralized decision-making process can enable an organization to proactively respond to changes in its external environment in a timely way.

Organizational structure is defined as the formal interactions of individuals and teams in the allocation of tasks, responsibilities, and authority to achieve the mission of the organization. The structure of an organization can help or hinder its progress toward accomplishing its purpose.

An organizational structure has two key roles in any NGO: it clarifies the role of each member, and it stipulates the degree of control each individual has. Even though organizational structures play an important function in an NGO, the same structures can create barriers between teams in different units of the NGO and between the NGO and its external stakeholders.

These barriers can inhibit teams from working together and make the organization less efficient and less receptive to the requirements of their targeted beneficiaries.

There are external and internal variables that influence the design or functionality of an NGO's internal structure. Organizational structures are dynamic because they are affected by constant changes in the environment.

ORGANIZATIONAL STRUCTURE TYPES

An NGO has to compare an organizational structure to its economic benefits. Traditional hierarchical structures are under pressure, and there is an increased preference for decentralization at operational and strategic levels.

Strategic flexibility, business diversification, and knowledge are needed in the current development scenario, and there is a need for intensive interaction among teams and external stakeholders.

The most appropriate organizational structure depends on the organization's purpose, the environment, the technology used, the degree, and frequency of change, the leadership style, and the size of the organization.

It is important to make sure that the structure selected is ideal based on the organization's size, program operations, and resources. The following are some structures that organizations adopt:

a. FUNCTIONAL ORGANIZATION STRUCTURE

The functional organization structure is the simplest structure. It groups individuals into units based on the roles they undertake. This could include the departments of finance, community relations, accounting, and human resource among others. It has line (chain of command) and staff (functional authority-experts) positions.

It is a hierarchical, usually vertically integrated organizational structure. Each unit consists of a separate role and the team has expertise in that field. It involves pooling individuals who share common professional competencies and responsibilities and a common approach in single-program organizations.

b. MATRIX ORGANIZATION STRUCTURE

The matrix organization structure is based on having experts from diverse functional groups work together to achieve a given project within a given budget and schedule. It is a combination of the traditional functional and product organization structures. It is suitable for organizations that have multiple projects.

This type of structure ensures that individuals with a wide range of skills will focus on a particular project or product and move quickly for results. The advantage of this arrangement is that the focus of the team members is on the purpose of project and the stakeholders. Decision making is decentralized, and the flexible utilization of resources and strong team coordination ensure a quick response to change.

Matrix structures are developed to manage ambiguity and changes within the environment. The structure provides for increased cooperation and communication among units and provides a quick response to technical problems and stakeholder demands. The potential for conflict is high in a matrix structure, as an employee may be required to report to two or more managers.

c. BOUNDARYLESS STRUCTURE

The boundaryless structure is one of the newer forms of organizational structures. It is an organization that is not defined by the horizontal, vertical, or external boundaries imposed by a defined structure.

It can involve the modular form (all nonessential functions are outsourced) or strategic alliances (a joint venture, with multiple NGOs identifying areas of collaboration). The structure is centered on relationships with other social organizations and organizations add value via relationships.

These are temporary organization structures formed to achieve a particular goal and once the goal is accomplished, the structure is dissolved. These structures help to deal with change more quickly. They allow communication and work to cross traditionally separate divisions of customers, suppliers, and even competitors.

This structure seeks to minimize or eliminate horizontal, vertical, and external limitations so that there are more interactions and sharing among employees and stakeholders. It is based on adaptive management approach.

The workforce engage in highly responsive and fluid approaches and such a structure requires individuals to be team players. Boundaryless structures need a stable vision and core values that enable individuals or teams within the organizations to emphasize collaboration on projects.

d. PRODUCT ORGANIZATION STRUCTURE

This structure is normally used when the organization sees a need to develop new products and services. It, therefore, means that each product or group of services becomes a separate unit. This structure is quite common in organizations that conduct research, product development, engineering and foundations. It involves temporary interdisciplinary teams, and organizations are structured by grouping people by task and profession.

The structure that an NGO adopts will vary; however, it is important that leadership understand that a structure will affect organizational performance and change. To achieve organizational goals and objectives, teams and individual employees need to be coordinated.

The type of structure an NGO selects should be tailored to the specific mission and goals it is trying to achieve. The changing environments of NGOs and the development sector create the need for developing new forms of organizing.

Organizational structures are often designed to reflect the level of growth of the organization. There are growth or lifecycle phases such as emergent, launch, consolidation, and, finally, maturity and each phase may require a different structure.

An effective structure supports an organization in understanding its leadership roles, and clarifies employee roles, responsibilities, and levels of authority.

Most local NGOs in developing countries are at different stages of development and growth and at different levels of capacity. The particular growth phase of an NGO may influence the organization's structure; therefore, it is important that the NGO's leadership understand that organizational structures when applicable need to be adjusted during each phase.

There is a close link between an NGO's strategy and the organizational structure it adopts. Structure is also is linked to workforce productivity and the NGO's overall performance.

It is crucial for NGOs to recognize that even though a particular structure may have been effective during the critical growth phases of the organization. However, once the environment changes the structure may no longer be suitable. This will require developing a different structure for the NGO to continue performing at an optimal level.

2. THE PRESENCE OF AN ADAPTIVE CULTURE

Culture gives an NGO an identity and the strength of the culture affects the NGO's effectiveness. Culture shapes organizational practices and performance and an NGO's ability to be adaptive and innovative is linked to its culture.

To promote sustainability, a local NGO needs to understand how culture develops, is managed, and changes to enhance the organization's influence and performance.

Traditional organizational cultures in the NGO sector continue to impede organizations' growth and unless local NGOs align themselves with current trends in organizational development and growth, they will continue to experience limitations.

It is often assumed that as an NGO matures, so does the culture of that organization. However, the challenge that local NGOs face is influencing or changing persistent and deep-rooted elements of culture such as ideals and philosophies that hinder performance.

Tangible and intangible levels of culture exist within organizations. Local NGOs have characters or dispositions just like people and they can be distant, rigid, cold, and unfavorable or flexible, supportive, and innovative. These traits or features of culture are sometimes very difficult to manipulate and manage to help foster an enabling environment in an organization.

Culture determines what takes place in an organization by defining what is important or unimportant in the organization. Culture is essential in the formation and alignment of organizational operations and the execution of tasks in an organization.

Culture is learned and it evolves within an organization through a maturing process. Owen, Mundy, Guild and Guild, [29] note that culture evolves over time and serves to guide the perception of what is essential (value), what is possible (opportunity), and what is real (reality). Hence, the set of beliefs become articulated through procedures that become normative and are sustained by the incentives and sanctions given by the organization.

An adaptive culture is a great basis for inspiration, increased performance and devotion amongst the board, management, and staff. An organization with an adaptive culture increases its performance and eventually its sustainability. An adaptive culture supports organizational flexibility and productivity especially with the dynamics of growth within an organization.

An adaptive culture facilitates the adoption of innovative initiatives that assist an NGO to seize opportunities in the external environment and to develop enterprising leaders.

For an NGO to succeed in its sustainability efforts, it must accomplish a mission that is esteemed and valued by both internal and external stakeholders.

An adaptive organizational culture helps to integrate and create synergy between the organization mission, processes, systems, and tasks. An NGO's prevailing culture can be the difference between growth and decline.

An NGO's culture needs to match the organizational purpose and mission if sustainability is to be achieved. The NGO's vision should be compelling and state the comprehensive changes the organization desires to achieve within society.

The organization's mission should give details of whom the NGO will target, their location, and the mechanisms of delivering their services. An organizational culture that is adaptive helps an NGO explore innovative ways to utilize its resources and carry out sustainable programs. Some actions that can be adopted to nurture an adaptive culture;

i. IDENTIFYING, DEVELOPING, AND TRACKING THE DESIRED CULTURE

It is important that the NGO develop and track cultural changes by reviewing whether the culture is aligned to the organization's vision, mission, and values, and whether there are barriers that need to be removed or minimized that would undermine the cultural ethos desired by the organization.

Where there is a steady adaptive culture, fundamental values are quickly embraced and employees relate to them. However, once employees get comfortable with a certain culture they develop a protective instinct, and resist change. Hence, a strong culture that binds people together to form non adaptive attitude can be catastrophic to an organization.

Secondly, where there is a weak culture, the opposite happens. Staff become individualistic, and the group is fragmented and hence less likely to have collective resistance. This minimizes barriers to structural change and an organization can introduce innovative techniques.

The above scenarios present how the culture of an organization affects performance and the management of human resources. A local NGO needs to consistently assess the culture of the organization if it is to continue providing quality services and products to ensure its relevance in the market.

A desired organizational culture is one that is flexible and solid enough to support external adaptation and internal integration. An NGO can use an organizational culture assessment tool to conduct an organizational culture mapping exercise.

Management and teams can identify the behaviors or attitude they would like to promote and then include those behavioral aspects in a performance appraisal tool, develop individual or team motivator strategies and orient or train staff at different levels within the organization on the attitudes and behaviors required to mold the desired culture.

ii. NURTURE A CAPTIVATING EMPLOYER BRAND

Sometimes individuals are reluctant to mention or identify with the organization they work for, or an NGO loses its talented employees within a short period, or there is a high number of cynics in the teams, the NGO lacks the diversity and balance it desires among its employees or it is consistently unable to attract the desired caliber of professionals required to fill in key positions. These scenarios point to the fact that the employer brand is weak.

The prevailing culture within an NGO shapes the way the organization does things, what it believes in, what it values, and what it rewards. Employer branding enables an organization to integrate its core values and beliefs, norms, and ideas that mold how an organization carries out its mission.

Employer branding is a strategic marketing initiative that attempts to make the organization an attractive place to work. A brand that is captivating helps to align to stakeholders' and clients' expectations and the reality within the organization.

Branding supports the desired organizational culture and needs to be adaptable to accommodate new work and personnel ethics. A local NGO needs to create a brand that is motivating to its workforce and one that nurtures an internal culture that employees can be proud of.

Employer branding helps an NGO establish suitable and appropriate organizational systems and processes to enable it to attract diverse resources and retain a positive relationship with its workforce.

Effective employer branding gives teams a sense of identity, inspires commitment and loyalty, increases employee satisfaction, and improves workforce productivity. This leads to the presence of organizational brand champions who are proud of what the local NGO stands for and this eventually reduces human resource costs.

Employer branding is crucial, as it helps an organization build a culture that attracts and retains people who are committed to achieving the NGO's mandates, thus helping build a high performance NGO.

A major task for organizational leadership is to promote the development of a captivating employer brand by using the employer brand excellence framework and fostering management attitudes that build a culture that makes the NGO a preferred employer.

3. PRESENCE OF A RESPONSIVE ORGANIZATIONAL STRATEGY

An NGO whose performance is low compared to its peers is at risk of losing its worth and in due course losing its competitive advantage. An NGO's goals and objectives define what it wants to undertake while strategy shows the how. Having a strategy is not a choice but a key component for an NGO's survival.

As NGOs grow, their structures, leadership, management, and operations must change to support the expansion. Developing an organizational strategy identifies and sets priorities, focuses resources, strengthens operations, establishes agreement around intended results, and adjusts the organization's focus.

An NGO needs to remain dynamic. However many local NGOs have lost the capacity and will to do so, and instead, are limited by inefficient practices and poor attitudes that hinder them from being proactive.

Effective strategic planning involves strategy formulation and execution. A strategy indicates where an NGO is going, documents the actions required to make progress, and, finally provides indicators that will measure success.

A strategy enables the NGO plan how to move from the present state to an envisioned future. This may involve an expansion of the organization's structure, diversification of services or resources, or more focus on stakeholders' expectation.

An NGO has to adapt to the internal and external environment by assessing and identifying challenges and opportunities that affect performance and sustainability. This assists the NGO in adequately addressing the evolving perceptions and expectations of stakeholders while staying abreast of the competition and proactively responding to social, political, technological and economic developments.

NGOs go through a life cycle that progresses through different phases. It is important for an organization to develop strategies to be adopted at each phase of its life, as the organization's objectives may vary at each phase. The phases are start-up, growth, maturity, and decline or transition phase. An NGO needs to develop organizational plans to enable it to navigate well through these phases to avoid stagnation or in the dissolution of the organization.

a. THE START-UP PHASE

During the start-up phase, the NGO's focus is getting off the ground. The organization has a small workforce, and the founders bear the responsibility of managing operations. Essential elements of strategy may include accessing adequate financing and establishing a presence in its sector of operation.

b. THE GROWTH PHASE

During the growth phase, the NGO seeks to maintain its services and operations to remain relevant in its sector of operation. The organization expands, and the founder can no longer manage all of the NGO's operations and roles.

The organization may choose a functional structure. Strategies involve having products or services in the market, building a consistent organization brand and creating partnerships and alliances with others in the defined market niche. For example, NGOs with limited resources can develop a niche strategy.

c. THE MATURITY PHASE

In the maturity phase, the NGO's brand is known, and the organization is recognized as the leader in its sector. The leadership seeks to maintain the organization's effectiveness, which may require hiring or downsizing of staff. The organizational structure becomes more divisional, with different departments emerging to address the NGO mission.

The NGO is mature and stable. It has a loyal stakeholder base, substantial resources through the diversification of funding streams, and a highly professional workforce. Strategies in the maturity phase are designed to increase competitiveness, introduce new services, enter new fields of opportunity, or re-evaluate the competencies of the workforce and assign them tasks that support the new focus.

d. THE DECLINE PHASE

In the decline phase, demand for an NGO's services starts reducing either steadily or rapidly. This can also be a period of stagnation, with no evidence of meaningful growth.

An NGO in the decline phase may lose its market to other NGOs with unique value propositions or superior services. A decline can occur after any of the phases not necessarily after maturity.

Organizational decline can be caused by organizational atrophy, clinging to obsolete technology, a decline in the customer base, fierce competition, an incompetent or reduced workforce, leadership challenges and inefficiencies in internal operations.

In the decline phase, organizational strategies can take two different approaches: an NGO can try to bounce back to the growth phase, or it can develop transition strategies, such as merging with another organization. Unfortunately, a decline is sometimes recognized when it is too late to recover, as early indications of stagnation are sometimes ignored or mistaken to be temporary.

The processes and systems that an NGO employs at each phase will determine the results and progress achieved during each phase of growth. Therefore, an NGO that seeks to obtain meaningful outcomes at each phase has to change or align its strategy, systems, and process with the envisioned results.

This requires a local NGO to be proactive to eliminate systems and process that are not aligned to the organizational goals and strategy through;

i.   use of a systems approach during strategy development;
ii. aligning strategy with organizational culture, with a focus on the drivers of results;

iii. incorporating change management, leadership, and employee development interventions;

iv. modifying or adopting new organizational elements that are vital for the NGO's growth;

v. developing actionable and measurable performance indicators; and

vi. incorporating learning to promote continuous improvement.

A strategy provides an NGO's leadership and management with a benchmark for measuring progress toward sustainability and organization performance.

4. EFFECTIVE ORGANIZATIONAL GOVERNANCE

Sustainable local NGOs are built on an empowering and open relationship between the organization's executive team and the board.

Governance is an important aspect for local NGOs, and organizations that ignore this aspect put long-term performance and the sustainability of the NGOs they serve at risk.

The following are elements that are key to ensuring effective governance to enhance NGO sustainability:

i. A FUNCTIONAL BOARD

NGO governance is the responsibility of board members and it goes beyond the board functions and responsibilities to include how members are selected and developed as well as how the board undertakes its operations to ensure decisions are productive and that the performance of the NGO is effective in furthering its mandate.

A functional board is key to the expansion and sustainability of local NGOs. An organization's sustainability relies on the composition and effectiveness of the NGO's board structure.

Individuals on a board are brought together to apply their experience and expertise to increase the organization's effectiveness and long term viability.

Board members should be responsible for their behavior and attitudes and it may be prudent to develop a member code of conduct to facilitate mutual accountability and build the board's team spirit.

A board should be guided by principles that help them understand their role and help them support the delivery of organizational purpose, develop team spirit, and foster integrity and accountability.

The principles can be summed up as accountability, fairness, transparency, and responsibility and they are designed to apply to all local NGOs. However, the NGO's actual practice and procedures may differ depending on the size and nature of the NGO.

ii. ACCOUNTABILITY MECHANISMS

Local NGOs are under constant pressure to demonstrate they are using resources in an effective manner. In many NGO project initiatives, compliance has been tied to accessing donor funds.

Compliance management helps an NGO develop effective internal accountability mechanisms. The NGO leadership is required to be assertive in learning about service delivery, country and donor policies, and technological changes reshaping the NGO and the development sector.

The board and management need to ensure the NGO complies with national and international laws and regulations, internal guidelines, agreements with donors, contracts, and reporting rules to enhance its competitive edge. This helps an NGO ensure it does not lose future income due to a bad image or reputation.

Boards should coordinate the setting up of self-regulatory mechanisms and ensure they are periodically assessed to determine effectiveness. The board and management team needs to monitor what must be changed or updated to meet stakeholder expectations and ensure that resources are used effectively.

Compliance can be further strengthened if the board and management builds support for achieving standards, provide mechanisms to make compliance achievable, and document performance information as it relates to progress toward compliance.

iii. MONITORING NGO GROWTH AND PERFORMANCE

Many NGOs underperform because their boards fail to undertake their key role of developing strategies that focus on the organization's growth and performance. Local NGO leadership needs to regularly review and monitor the "fit" between the decisions the organization makes and what the organization stands for.

A board needs to advance from low-level tasks that create feelings of frustration and underutilization among board members to addressing key tasks that are strategic. This will entail four basic elements:

1. Involvement in strategic issues that are key to NGO performance.
2. Be guided by outcomes that are linked to defined strategic goals and timeliness.
3. The presence of clear measurements of success.
4. Solicitation of feedback on the NGO's performance or growth from the organization's internal and external stakeholders.

An NGO board has to proactively monitor the NGO's growth and performance within its sector and region of operation. A board should ideally build the capacity of the NGO's workforce through its board members' expertise.

5. EMBRACING AN INTEGRATED CHANGE MANAGEMENT APPROACH

If a local NGO desires to improve its performance or make any progress, change is inevitable. For an NGO to remain competitive, it is required to make changes. However, in many local NGOs most change efforts fail to yield anticipated results due to staff resistance, poorly formulated initiatives, and inadequate management support.

Change within an organization may involve adjustments in an NGO's strategy, structure, procedures, policies, employees, technology, or culture. Organizational change can be extreme and quickly change the way an organization functions or it may involve incremental adjustments.

Local NGOs must adapt to changes that enable them to achieve sustained growth and survive for an extended period. NGOs need to respond quickly to the local, national, and global changes that introduce new technologies and competition if they want to survive.

Local NGOs have to understand and appreciate that organizations are made up of human beings, with values, beliefs, hopes, and fears. Organizations need to be careful not to ignore the predictable or unpredictable individual reactions that will obviously undermine a change initiative in the future. Therefore, managing the people side of any change initiative is crucial.

Change management is a structured organizational process that seeks to transition organizations from the present status to the desired future, to help in the realization of the organizational vision and mission.

Change management enables NGOs to systematically adopt and effect changes to address community or sector needs. Change management can be viewed as a systematic approach, transitioning process or a competitive strategy.

i) A SYSTEMATIC APPROACH

It is a precise or logical process that seeks to bring about a shift or adjustment in an NGO's operating structures. It involves outlining and endorsing an organization's approaches, systems, and processes to handle change resulting from prevailing internal and external situations.

ii) A TRANSITION PROCESS

It is an approach that includes a set of activities that help individuals or organizations adopt new structures, processes, values, and technologies. It helps individuals or organizations embrace new ways of undertaking actions to achieve the desired state.

iii) A COMPETITIVE STRATEGY

It is a continuous process of adjusting or re-aligning an organization within its niche or sector of operation so that it can be more responsive and effective than its competitors.

External or internal aspects can provoke changes within a local NGO. However, for a change initiative to succeed within an organization, it must be carried by a vision. A vision clarifies the direction that the change will take and developing a strategy provides a roadmap that will ensure that the vision is achieved.

Effective change management helps individuals within organizations to work collectively toward a common defined goal that in the end will help the NGO to realize benefits and deliver results.

There is increased demand for building internal change management competencies as opposed to relying on external actors. Organizations that fail to learn from errors become vulnerable to predictable surprises.[30]

NGOs need to embrace change to be sustainable because stakeholder demands continue to grow, and technologies are evolving. If the existing culture within an organization is in alignment with the proposed changes then that culture will accelerate the implementation of the change initiatives.

It is important that a local NGO's leadership recruit committed and respected individuals who have authority and influence to guide change initiatives at their level.

Factors that cause change efforts in most local NGOs to fail are inadequate leadership focus on the complexity of the change initiative, lack of a change strategy and structures and paying minimal attention to individual behaviors toward the change program being initiated.

THE IMPORTANCE OF AN NGO HAVING THE CAPACITY TO EMBRACE CHANGE

An organization that desires to be effective requires its leaders to re-align its design, culture, and people with continuous changes in the competitive environment.[31]

For change to be effective there is a need for commitment, structures, resources and processes to support the change initiatives. A local NGO risks the following if it has no capacity to manage change:

i. a decline in NGO and staff productivity.
ii. the deterioration of staff morale and high turnover of valued employees.
iii. an inability to meet deadlines for projects and to undertake them within the stipulated budgets.
iv. increase in passive resistance among employees as individuals find avenues to avoid the new ways of accomplishing tasks or revert to the old processes.
v. the organization experiences repeated failures of its change programs or efforts.
vi. the loss of opportunities in the market space or niche.
vii. the development of a "not-invented-here" syndrome that eventually leads to a lack of organizational absorptive capacity.

RESPONDING EFFECTIVELY TO CHANGE

Organizations need to consider the following to respond effectively to change:

i. Create urgency for the change envisioned.
ii. Develop a vision and strategy to manage the change initiative.
iii. Explore the organization's value structure and change capacity.
iv. Be aware of the degree of resistance.
v. Consider the expected changes anticipated from the change action.
vi. Who or what is the focus of the envisioned change? That is the groups, systems or structures to be impacted.
vii. Consider the type and amount of change in relation to the timeframe.
viii. Develop a change communication plan.
ix. Consider the expertise that exists.
x. Consider the organization's past change history.
xi. Manage the emotions that come with the changes.

xii.   Build employee and stakeholder commitment to change.
xiii. Identify change processes that have an overall impact on the NGO business.
xiv.   Set aside resources to support change management initiatives.
xv.   Follow through and institutionalize change initiatives.

Effective change management will assist NGOs in integrating and aligning people, processes, and culture with the overall organization's strategy. Local NGOs therefore require leadership and management attitudes that motivate, foster and build commitment and a shared purpose to support the implementation of change initiatives within the organization.

Leaders execute change by formulating a vision, influencing the acceptance of organizational goals, providing support at an individual level and consistently clarifying performance expectations.

The process used to design change initiatives especially their prioritization, and the individuals involved in their design are crucial to the actual implementation of change. Having a systematic approach to prioritizing change initiatives and involving key influencers or relevant individuals across the organization during the design process is more likely to yield success in the implementation of a change initiative.

6. ADOPTION OF STRATEGIC HR MANAGEMENT PRACTICES

Human resources are an essential NGO asset that provides a sustained competitive advantage. They provide a link to the achievement of an NGO's strategic goal and its strategic positioning endeavors.

People are an important aspect in all social organizations. The importance of people is immense, because they are instrumental in developing the organization's objectives and achievements attained. [32]

One of the most common human resource (HR) practices in local NGOs is to focus on people first, then on roles. This means organizations select individuals for positions before the roles are fully defined. This is disruptive and distracting for an NGO that seeks to enhance its performance.

From the perspective of the organization, people are resources and organizations cannot exist without them, as they are important for survival. However, local NGOs need to align team and individual performances to sustain the organization's vision and mission. This can be achieved by adopting strategic human resource management practices.

A strategic approach to HR ensures that all departments have the ability to recruit required talent to fill each position in the structure in a transparent and systematic way, so that competent individuals are placed in crucial roles.

Strategic human resource management is an approach that defines how the organization's goals will be achieved through people by means of human resource strategies and integrated HR policies and practices.[33]

There are four generic human resource strategies used in different contexts, as follows:

i. Talent acquisition and management strategy focuses on getting the best human talent from within and without.
ii. Resource allocation strategy desires to maximize the engagement of current human resources by ensuring the appropriate individuals are in the right positions.
iii. A talent improvement plan focuses on continuous training and guiding career development of employee in their jobs.
iv. A cost reduction strategy that focuses on lowering personnel costs.

Local NGOs need to recognize that to be successful they must critically look into recruiting competent and skilled staff. Strategic HRM is a process that can assist local NGOs to systematically link employees and organizational strategic focus.

The focus is on aligning human resource practices, policies, and programs with strategic plans of the NGO.

Integration between HRM and an organization's strategic plan contributes to the effective management of human resources and improve the organization's performance.[34] A crucial aspect for local NGO leadership is to evaluate the extent to which strategic integration and devolvement are adopted within organizations.

Local NGOs need to recognize that the staff, the organization's HR systems and practices are important factors in securing a sustainable competitive advantage in their market space or niche.

Some strategies that can help local NGOs adopt strategic HRM practices include the following:

i. DEVELOPING A HRM STRATEGY

A strategy will help link the strategic focus of the organization to human resource needs. It will align the HR function and role directly to the organization's strategic plan. This builds a strategic approach to handling an organization's important human resources.

NGO strategies and approaches to implementation change and evolve over time. Local NGO staff are required to be familiar with the future of the organization and their future in the organization. This helps to activate commitment and hence sustained productivity.

Developing a strategy will involve understanding from a human resource management perspective the link between the human resource required and the NGO's vision. This requires reviewing the organization's mission, existing and proposed departments, and all the existing staff categories. This also involves analyzing changes in the external environment and matching human resources to strategic organizational goals.

The developed plan identifies the gaps that need to be filled to improve HR systems and practices. The plan also highlights the competencies required in the present and future that will enable the organization to achieve its objectives.

Some questions that can help to link HR strategy and the overall organizational strategy:

a. What are the human resource gaps or opportunities being advanced by the NGO's vision and mission?
b. What human resource gaps and opportunities are being advanced by the NGO's desired values?

c. What human resource gaps and opportunities are advanced by the envisioned strategic actions or goals explored in the scenario planning?

d. What are the key human resource gaps or opportunities related to the current or future actions needed for strategic positioning?

e. What action plans and resources are required to address the gaps and opportunities?

A HRM strategy enables an NGO to systematically link the performance of employees and organizational strategic focus.

ii. USING COMPETENCY MAPPING AND SUCCESSION PLANNING TO DEVELOP STAFF CAPACITY

The staff's unwavering respect and commitment to the organization's mandates and values ensures successful achievement of the local NGO's objectives. It is important for the NGO's leadership and management to realize that the current staffing competence may be different from the staffing required to implement future NGO program goals and its overall mission.

A local NGO's performance and continuity requires the organization to have qualified and sufficient employees in place to support the implementation of identified organizational strategies and tasks.

Competency mapping ensures that the NGO has the human resource talent and skills required to achieve its goals and deliver results effectively in the present and in the future.

Succession planning is a deliberate management decision to build and stimulate the continuous availability of adequate staff and to make sure that key staff positions have some degree of stability or permanence.

Succession planning assists NGO leadership and management ensure that essential expertise and capacities are retained when a staff member in an indispensable position exits.

Competency mapping helps teams develop succession plans that are linked to the strategic focus of the organization. The practices of competency mapping and succession planning are now no longer only at the executive level but also at other levels within the organization. Mapping and succession planning help management to:

a. understand positions, that if abolished or redesigned will have an impact on the organization's objectives or those that may need to be incorporated to improve performance;
b. ensure there is a steady supply of talent within the organization to respond to the changing realities of workplaces;
c. identify and explore strategies to develop the expertise and capacity of the human resources available;
d. coordinate and plan the workforce;
e. support a culture of knowledge transfer and development of potential staff to fill critical positions.

Competency mapping and succession planning practices assist an NGO in being proactive in coordinating and managing its workforce.

iii. DEVELOPING A CULTURE OF FACILITATIVE SUPERVISION

Successful local NGOs need to recognize the significance of staff performance in the organization's success. This requires NGOs to focus their supervision efforts on development and motivation of staff.

Supervision at many NGOs tends to emphasize inspection and control or intimidation as management view staff as unmotivated and lacking the skills to perform their tasks. At the same time, the managers or leaders have inadequate competencies to support employee performance. This means the managers and leaders focus more on problem solving that is reactive and sporadic.

Local NGOs need to put effort into supporting employees through developing an empowering approach for monitoring and providing performance feedback to employees.

The purpose of facilitative supervision is to empower staff to get more involved in problem-solving by taking initiatives to get work done and improve the quality of service.

A facilitative supervision culture nurtures productive and professional employees who have the required competencies to work consistently to achieve the organization's mission. This results in high performance NGO that has the capacity to sustain its growth.

Facilitative supervision is viewed as an integrated approach that provides ongoing performance monitoring and quality improvement. It can include one on one meetings, site visits, or individual staff reviews.

The facilitative supervision approach links organization's strategies to individual performance efforts and helps to enhance the employee's competencies to perform effectively. Facilitative supervision enables management measure performance and give on- going feedback that provides the workforce with information that helps them manage their performance.

Effective management of human resource determines the ongoing performance and survival of the organization. An effective facilitative supervision approach helps the leadership and management to identify and allocate the required resources to assist employees in effectively performing their tasks.

Ideally every individual has the capacity and the ability to perform but the individual will only excel in an environment that has in place systems and structures that motivate performance.

7. ACHIEVING QUALITY IN PROGRAM DELIVERY

Organizations that focus on quality tend to be more sustainable because they perceive quality as a process and not an event. These organizations therefore, seek to continuously meet their stakeholders' expectations and needs by developing and monitoring compliance to standards.

However, many local NGOs do not bother to maintain the quality of their program operations as the organization's founders or management do not see the need or do not have the expertise or skills to spearhead the process.

Some strategies to help local NGOs achieve excellence in program delivery include the following:

i. DEFINING PURPOSE TO MAXIMIZE EFFECTIVENESS.

Developing a project plan is a good management practice, but sometimes the actual project implementation process is wanting. This occurs because the project implementation plan fails to incorporate the envisioned future and the expectations of the stakeholders.

In other instances, the project plan's focus is on the mission of the NGO and it fails to take into consideration what the organization encounters at the grassroot or community level.

Local organizations that develop long-term plans that align to the NGO's mission and address the needs of the communities targeted will deliver quality services that are sustainable. This is because all priorities and targets tie back to strategic plan goals.

Organizations need to pursue strategic and sustainable opportunities to achieve excellence in project implementation and, as a result, achieve the NGO's mandate. This requires selecting projects that are in sync with the organization's available resources, capabilities and deliver the most value to the organization.

A local NGO needs to determine if it is effectively utilizing its available resources by realigning its services or projects to the NGO's mission.

An outcome-oriented approach to providing services is an important element to look into. This means the focus is on the change that the organization desires to see as a result of its services or programs. The anticipated changes need to be aligned to the organization's mandate and strategic focus.

An analysis of the existing competition is important in developing a strong strategic position. This helps an NGO to understand what other NGOs are offering and doing, and this assists an organization in making strategic decisions to become more effective and efficient in the delivery of services.

ii. RESPOND TO BENEFICIARIES OR COMMUNITY NEEDS.

A local NGO needs to be continuously aware of its community's present and emerging needs to maximize resources available and services. If the NGO's mission runs parallel to community needs, it results in dissatisfaction with the services and the NGO risks losing credibility among its key stakeholders. An NGO's sustainability is often tied to the nature and quality of services it consistently provides at the community level. Local NGOs must have quality assurance procedures that monitor services provided to communities to ensure quality is not compromised over time.

An organization has to have unique services that should not be confused with those of another organization. An NGO that does not effectively identify and implement interventions that respond to beneficiaries' needs runs the risk of duplicating the services of another organization. This will mean demand for the services will be minimal or reduced overtime and it will become difficult to sustain projects initiated at community level.

A viable local NGO provides an avenue for the needs of vulnerable communities to be heard in policy-making processes. This entails having political support from government structures and aligning interventions to policies at the local level.

However, this is only applicable if an NGO has the competency and capacity to assess and accurately understand the situation from the perspective of those who are vulnerable and design appropriate responses.

Local NGOs need to create community structures that create demand for services and also have in place community champions at grassroot level with good negotiating skills.

iii. ADOPTION OF PROJECT MANAGEMENT PRACTICES

The changing nature of development practice has resulted in the introduction of various methodologies in undertaking development initiatives that demand different capabilities from staff. This calls for the ability to work as a "reflective practitioner."

Most local NGOs face challenges from having unrealistic project plans; inadequate stakeholder involvement; inadequate skills to identify project risks, analyze opportunities and inadequate skills to manage project budgets just to mention a few. This results in massive project failures and stakeholder dissatisfaction with the project outcomes.

The ability of an NGO to undertake successful projects is determined by their capacity to increasingly utilize project management techniques that enable it to design local innovative solutions that address the identified need while still meeting the organization's mandate. Project management techniques and tools help the NGO align its programmatic, social, institutional, and financial objectives to the prevailing circumstances.

Project management skills are important, as they will assist the project team in planning, implementing, and monitoring project activities to meet the project's objectives.

Local NGOs need an integrated approach that integrates projects within the existing organizational system so that interventions remain part of the organizational activities even after donor funds are reduced or project staff exit. This calls for organizations to ensure that project objectives are in alignment with their overall strategy and mandates.

iv. MANAGING MONITORING AND EVALUATION AS A LEARNING PROCESS

The function of monitoring and evaluation (M and E) is knowledge generation; however, in most local NGOs, the presence of outdated practices continues to hinder the utilization of learning-oriented innovations in program delivery.

The idea of learning and the importance of facilitating learning within project teams is well recognized but sadly, learning is seen as simply training by many in the development field.

Most development organizations have informal monitoring mechanisms to manage activity implementation. However, there is a need for innovative systems that enable reflection for purposes of learning and gathering knowledge from internal and external stakeholders to improve service delivery within projects.

A structured process of reflection and documentation on experiences of selected development activity is therefore crucial. Where local NGOs effectively manage M and E as a learning process it enhances their capability to explore the development of project outputs or outcomes into new opportunities for projects or for establishing new networks.

8. DEVELOPING STRATEGIES FOR MANAGING COLLABORATIONS

High performance NGOs will be those that nurture long-term relationships with donors and other stakeholders by providing greater opportunities for involvement and value creation. Local NGOs have to demonstrate how donor investment creates a sustainable impact on the beneficiaries it serves.

Partnerships go through phases during which certain strategies are important to ensure local NGOs receive the maximum mutual benefits from engagements. Local NGOs need to be strategic and collaborate with other stakeholders who add value to their ongoing projects.

NGOs need to create and maintain enabling conditions that will help them manage collaborations with others. Outstanding performance depends on the existence of strong relations and mutual trust with other key stakeholders.

Local NGOs need to strategically invest in establishing and maintaining strong relationships with their key external stakeholders. This is because relations within a collaboration or partnership require balancing between "psychological" contracts and the formal legal contracts.

The following are some aspects that NGOs can work on to manage their collaborations or partnerships to create greater value;

I. FOSTER TRUST AMONG STAKEHOLDERS

Long-term relationships require a lot of efforts in building and maintaining trust throughout the partnership lifecycle. Trust is important in partnerships to ensure successful relationships, and local NGOs need to prove that they can deliver on their promises. Organizations need to consistently demonstrate to other stakeholders and organizations that they can be trusted. The following are some categories of trust that organizational relationships may be built on:

1. DETERRENCE BASED TRUST

When an NGO does what it says it will do, it helps in managing expectations, establishing clear boundaries or scope, delegating appropriately and honoring agreements. This can be compared to contractual-based trust, where guidelines are put in place to prevent one team from taking advantage of the other. Relationships at this level are fragile, and there is not much disclosure.

2. KNOWLEDGE-BASED TRUST

Knowledge based trust is built on what the NGO knows about the other organization. It is trust that relies on information. It is based on the predictability of the behavior of the other entity and grows out of a history of previous engagement. This belief is based on the knowledge gained of the other entity.

3. IDENTIFICATION-BASED TRUST

In identification-based trust there is an emotional connection between the partners. Relations at this level involve honesty and disclosure. This involves sharing difficult truths, receiving and giving constructive feedback. Minimal controls are present at this level. There is minimal monitoring of the other entity within the partnership.

4. COMPETENCE-BASED TRUST

This involves respecting teammates on the basis of competency and skills and requires building an individual NGO's own expertise as well as helping others learn new skills. This level of trust is established once the partner has proved they are capable.

Trust falters when there are violations of the above four aspects of trust. It is difficult to determine the impact of violations or questionable behavior, but it usually affects levels of trust.

Trust requires an element of courage and commitment to believe that the other stakeholders will play their part. Organizations prove they are worthy of a partnership engagement through acts of consistency, competence, commitment, and integrity.

II. DEVELOPING AND MAINTAINING RELATIONS

Many local NGOs, once they have signed collaboration agreements, contracts or memorandum of understanding (MOUs) with other stakeholders they forget to focus on relationship maintenance. Developing and maintaining relations with stakeholders an NGO is working with is important and may involve the following:

A. LEVEL ONE (BUILD)

During initiation and planning phase, the NGO may need to:

   i. Acknowledge the NGOs' community histories and partnership experiences.

  ii. Acknowledge and appreciate the expertise of other NGOs or stakeholders.

 iii. Be upfront on expectations and intentions.

 iv. Understand the context of the partnership project.

  v. Listen to the NGOs to understand what they know and what works.

B. LEVEL TWO (MAINTAIN)

During the implementation, maintenance and transition phases in a partnership, NGOs need to keep in mind the following:

   i. Never assume that people or other stakeholders know the approach of the partnership or the individual NGO. There is need for ongoing awareness of the partnership and its interventions to keep NGO members' interest.

  ii. Revisit steps three, four and five in level one (BUILD).

 iii. Ensure that the NGO matches words with actions as this reinforces the idea that the NGO understands the issue, the project benefits users, there is joint working in all partnership phases, and efforts are being made to continue the program.

III. STRATEGIES FOR NURTURING DIFFERENT TYPES OF COLLABORATION

It is crucial, in addition to building trust and maintaining relations with other stakeholders that an NGO is aware that different types of collaborations require different strategies for sustaining them:

i. TRANSACTIONAL OR NEED-BASED RELATIONS

Transactional relations are formed with a focus on direct material gain for each organization involved. What holds the entities together are the services provided. Therefore, maintaining this relationship means that efforts focus on ensuring that the arrangement fulfills each entity's needs or expectations through:

a) Communicating regularly on any situational changes that may adversely affect the agreement.

b) Scheduling meetings with partners or stakeholders to discuss how the current working arrangements are progressing or achieving the changes required.

ii. COMPLEMENTARY OR OPPORTUNITY BASED RELATIONS

Complementary relations are formed by organizations with compatible missions and may be targeting the same users or communities. It involves harnessing and exploring each other as referral sources or jointly working on community initiatives.

Therefore, maintaining this relationship involves each partner exploring and identifying new opportunities for collaborations. It includes:

a) Continuously seeking new opportunities to jointly work on projects that bring value to each organization.

b) Communication that is more intensive than in the transactional partnership.

c) Scheduling quarterly meetings for joint sharing and learning, even if new initiatives are not available.

iii. COLLABORATIVE MISSION AND VISION BASED RELATIONS

Mission and vision based relations integrate the partners into each other's day-to-day operations, yet the individual organizations remain independent. The goal is to work jointly to achieve a common vision and entities exert considerable influence on each other.

Maintenance is determined by the partners' satisfaction with the collaborative focus and the relations between them. It involves:

a) Scheduling regular sessions to discuss the maintenance of a common vision and eliminate any barriers that may hinder accomplishing the vision.

b) Establishing structures and systems for bonding and managing the team dynamics because in such a partnership relationships are key.

Developing strategic approaches to managing partnerships will help local NGOs expand their circles of collaborations and enhance the survival rates of start-up local NGOs. A local NGO that wants to succeed in maintaining its partnerships to gain a competitive advantage and sustained performance needs to do the following:

a) Develop a partnership strategy. An organization cannot collaborate with everyone. There is need to be focused on the how and who to collaborate with. Organizations can categorize their partnerships at three levels strategic, operational, and transactional. Each requires different tactics to be developed and sustained.

b) Build partnerships on set principles and understand the expectations and agenda of the other entity in order to build trust.

c) Periodically monitor the direction and relevance of existing partnership engagements. It is important to measure outcomes that reflect critical factors that will build up the NGO's competitiveness.

d) There is need to develop facilitative leadership when managing partnerships as this helps in maintaining a high level of trust.

e) Ensure equity in the partnership by building individual NGO competencies and capacity to contribute to the creation of value in an engagement.

9. ORGANIZATIONAL LEARNING

Learning occurs internally and externally within the operating boundaries of an organization. However, many NGOs fail to capture the learning because they do not realize that before organizations are able to improve performance, individuals and organizations must learn.

Organizational learning is a dynamic process that relies on organizational and individual capabilities. Organizational learning is said to occur when an NGO's actions change through embracing new knowledge and practices.

In the current development sector, with the many complexities of undertaking development initiatives, changing donors and government priorities an NGO must learn from current and past experiences or learn from other like-minded organizations or adapt relevant best practices from other sectors to gain a competitive advantage or improve performance.

Local NGOs must be agile and operate profitably in an increasingly competitive environment. The learning capacity of an organization for improvement and competitiveness cannot be underestimated.[35] A local NGO will experience great gains if it can increase its knowledge utilization by a small fraction.

Learning helps an NGO in its innovation efforts, and for an NGO to survive and develop, it is necessary to engage in continuous learning. Organizational learning can take place for two purposes:

i. SINGLE LOOP LEARNING

The aim is to correct and adjust practices to align them with a developed policy.

ii. DOUBLE LOOP LEARNING

The aim is to expand the organization's ability to stimulate creative thinking so that the organization can implement innovatively.

ORGANIZATIONAL LEARNING ASPECTS

Organizational learning occurs when an NGO can generate, possess, and transfer knowledge to modify its behaviors and to reflect new organizational perspectives.

An NGO's continued success depends on learning at the individual level, yet many organizations do not understand the process and value of learning.

Not much thought is given to the contributions individuals make to knowledge creation within local NGOs. Organizational learning can be divided into three main areas:

a) LEARNING BEFORE

Learning before takes place before a project, or an organization is initiated. The focus is on learning from other individuals and identifying practical suggestions or solutions from past lessons or promising practices.

b) LEARNING DURING

This takes place while a project is being undertaken or an organization is expanding. The focus is on continuously monitoring and assessing the organization's strategy, capacity, project objectives, and the extent which it is achieving its mission.

c) LEARNING AFTER

This takes place after project completion or an organization has reached a stagnation period, or the occurrence of transition. The focus is on having a structure for reflection, development of action items and future replication of lessons.

STRATEGIES TO SUPPORT THE ADOPTION OF LEARNING PRACTICES

The rapidly changing environment and the changing nature of development approaches demand that local NGOs develop the capacity to constantly learn from practice and the experiences of others.

Many times when organizations fail, they ignore and lack the ability to learn from the implementation of projects or initiatives. Therefore, NGOs that desire to be sustainable cannot fail to embrace learning.

The way organizations structure learning reveals the existing perceptions or values they have on the learning agenda. Many organizations do not see learning as a strategic activity; hence they give it little attention even when developing an organizational strategic plan.

The following strategies can assist local NGOs in adopting learning as a continuous practice;

i. DEVELOPING A CULTURE OF LEARNING

In many local NGOs, the management and leadership emphasize on action rather than reflection processes. The excuse is often that staff are overloaded with urgent tasks and hence do not have time to engage in reflective processes.

In many local NGOs, the "cause" takes priority over reflection whenever there is a choice. Unfortunately, this has resulted in many local NGOs losing to their competitors as their services or operations have not been aligned to internal and external stakeholder expectations.

An organization's capacity to learn from experience and translate ideas into action is important to having a sustained competitive advantage.[36]When staff feel safe, they are free to express their ideas, and organizations are more likely to learn from experience. Therefore, a culture of safety is noted to facilitate learning.

Organizational learning and reflection initiatives produce positive effects provided the right approach is taken. In NGOs where learning initiatives are implemented in a structured and systematic manner, the organization experiences sustained growth in its operations.

Delay in providing feedback hinders individuals' learning from experience. When employees' actions do not receive immediate rewards or sanctions then learning within the organization is hindered.

Employees need to be exposed to learning events and link the learning with actual practice. Adequate resources are required to support and promote organization-wide learning and inter- organizational learning events.

ii. ADOPTING PROMISING PRACTICES THROUGH BENCHMARKING

Local NGOs sometimes lack the courage to unlearn practices that hinder growth in the organization. This is because some individuals or teams are comfortable with outdated practices that do not add value.

Learning can be a painful process because it sometimes involves unlearning perceptions that individuals or teams have had for a long time. Unlearning requires releasing what is known so as to provide a clean slate for new learning to take place which is a difficult thing for many individuals and organizations.

Local NGOs can use internal and external benchmarking approaches to enable them enhance learning among their teams. This can be done by developing indicators to track learning by comparing their progress with that of other NGOs who use good practices.

Bench marking is a continuous process that is structured. There are four types of benchmarking processes; internal, external, functional and generic or process benchmarking.

A bench marking process should not be seen as an inflexible approach, but it should be viewed as a process that guides and encourages the exploration of new ideas or innovations to enhance learning.

Continuous reflection on organizational internal practices and operations often leads to the improvement of the NGO's performance and knowledge base. It becomes difficult for an NGO to market itself or improve its services if it does not engage systematic learning processes.

iii. THE LEADERSHIP STYLE OF MANAGEMENT

Leaders have a role in building behaviors and attitudes that will enhance organizational learning. Where a management team micro manages staff and undermines their decisions learning and performance are hindered.

Leaders sometimes resist learning initiatives because they have built their careers on control vested in vertical structures while learning builds on horizontal structures that encourage sharing across the organizations.

When management does not have positive approaches to managing failure or success then minimal or no learning occurs. There are three organizational or leadership responses to failure and success that affect the adoption of new attitudes, practices or behaviors:

a. THE SELF-DECEIVING RESPONSE

This views failure or success as a mistake. The error or success is hidden, and if it is an error, someone is left with all the blame. If it is a success, the leader takes all the credit. Such responses mean that minimal learning will occur at the organizational and individual levels.

b. THE DEFEATED RESPONSE

Failure or success is viewed as a force beyond control. The failure or success is discussed in depth, but no action is taken. This response tends to leave an organization at crossroads with little improvement in organizational practices or individual attitudes. It leads to an attitude of business as usual among the employees or organization.

c. THE LEARNING RESPONSE

Error or success is viewed as a source of data, evidence, or information. The failure or success is discussed openly to understand the factors that led to the outcome. If it was an error, then corrective actions are attempted. And if it was a success, the action is institutionalized for greater results. The result is that employees are empowered to reflect and learn from previous encounters and to advance new practices.

iv. UNDERSTANDING THE LINK BETWEEN KM AND OL

Organizational learning (OL) has to do with institutionalization of what has been learned into the organization. Organizational learning complements knowledge management.[37]

The focus of organizational learning is the process while the focus of KM is content of the knowledge that an NGO obtains, develops, refines, and finally utilizes.

Organizational learning, therefore, involves developing, preserving, and transmitting of knowledge within an NGO. Local NGOs are required to put more effort toward developing capacity in the learning and knowledge management dimensions.

10. A STRATEGIC APPROACH TO RESOURCE DEVELOPMENT

Local NGOs need adequate and stable funding to continue undertaking their community development projects. However, one dangerous trap that local NGOs fall into is assuming that the present supply of income will remain constant and that previous resource mobilization strategies will remain effective and productive in the present and future scenarios.

Unfortunately, in the development sector, a lot of competition has emerged from other stakeholders who compete for the same donor resources. Therefore, an NGO's success in accessing resources will depend on the organization's knowledge and expertise in raising funds.

According to Batti,[38] NGOs for a long time have relied on the generosity of donors to support their project activities through grants and donations. However, local NGOs have now realized that such funding sources are never sufficient to address community's emerging needs and project implementation costs.

STRATEGIES FOR RESOURCE DEVELOPMENT

Some strategies that can help local NGOs expand or grow in resource development include the following:

i. DEVELOPING A RESOURCE MOBILIZATION PLAN AND STRATEGY

A strategy provides a roadmap that details what resources are needed and how they will be sourced. The resource mobilization action plan is tied to the annual plan of the organization, while the resource strategy is an organization wide and linked to the strategic direction of the organization.

There are conventional and non-conventional mechanisms to source funds or resources to support NGO interventions. It is therefore, important for local NGOs to identify mechanisms they have not fully explored and design strategies to access the available resources.

NGOs are required to envision where they desire to be and develop a plan that helps them access resources that will help them tackle and deal with the identified needs of the targeted group or community. In developing the strategy, two aspects are important:

a) UNDERSTANDING THE RESOURCE MOBILIZATION CYCLE
The cycle assists an NGO in identifying, designing, planning, and monitoring its resource mobilization initiatives. It entails the following actions:

  i.   Initial appraisal and planning.
  ii. Action or implementation.
  iii. Monitoring progress on strategy implementation.
  iv. Reviewing the lessons learned and revising the strategy.

b) MAPPING POTENTIAL RESOURCE PROVIDERS
Local NGOs that desire to be sustainable need to diversify their resource mobilization mechanisms to accommodate options of sourcing resources from diverse stakeholders.

There are many resource providers around the world and within Africa, who have the capability to provide resources based on their organizational targets and objectives. The key to identifying potential resource providers is in understanding their objectives and what they provide and for how long.

The assessment of resource providers is an ongoing process and local NGOs need to understand the current or emerging focus of the potential resource providers. Local NGOs need to identify and focus on providers with whom they share similar missions, goals, and objectives. This helps the team to explore and determine the mechanisms required to mobilize the prospective donors.

Therefore, the strategy and action plan are two important documents that NGOs need to have to enable them to continuously diversify their resource base.

ii. LEADERSHIP'S INVOLVEMENT IN RESOURCE MOBILIZATION

Resource mobilization is a strategic process that needs to be spearheaded at the executive level. Local NGOs need to refocus and appreciate that organizations must mobilize both financial and non-financial resources to build the NGO's sustainability.

DiMattia,[39] emphasizes the importance of having someone at the top with the belief, energy, and time to spearhead fundraising efforts. Therefore, resource mobilization capacity among the NGO leadership, especially the board and management, is critical in helping the organization achieve sustainability.

Organizations that want to be strategic in resource mobilization cannot ignore the issues of competition. It is important for an organization's board members to lead the team to assess its environment to know whether their programs and services are clearly different from what similar organizations are doing.

This is a critical board function that needs to be strengthened to assist an NGO in sourcing the resources required to enhance its performance and sustainability.

11. SOUND FINANCIAL GOVERNANCE

Many NGOs, as they expand, will have to enter into alliances or partnerships with other organizations to exploit greater markets or meet the stakeholders' growing demands hence the need to manage the strategic aspects of finance.

An important segment of sustainability planning is to plan to have sufficient resources and become self-reliant. This may be an achievable or realistic goal for some local NGOs who have the capacity to self-generate funds to cover overhead costs.

Some strategies that can be used by local NGOs to nurture sound financial governance practices include the following:

i. DEVELOPING A FINANCING ROADMAP

NGOs in developing nations are competing with other institutions for resources from diverse stakeholders. The competition is stiff, and sometimes an NGO is not always successful in the process. Due to this frustration with the funding and the pressure to decrease donor dependency, a local NGO must develop a financing plan that will guide how the organization intends to fund its activities.

A financing strategy gives an NGO some autonomy from a single donor or funding mechanism. A financing strategy highlights how the organization intends to finance its operations to meet strategic goals. This may include exploring different funding streams (restricted and unrestricted), building financial reserves, generating income, developing policies to support the strategy, reducing percentage of donor funds, replacing and maintaining fixed assets, and managing the NGO's financial overhead.

Local NGOs need adequate financial management practices that will help them develop multi-year financial projections to assist in long term planning and grant management. This allows an NGO to analyze hidden costs and patterns so that it can make appropriate adjustments to improve its financial performance in the future. This involves adopting plan based resource allocation strategies.

A financing strategy helps an organization enhance its autonomy as it enables an organization decline resources that are not aligned to its mission, pay competitive salaries to its staff and ensures provision of quality services.

ii. PRESENCE OF APPROPRIATE INTERNAL CONTROL FRAMEWORK

Experience has shown that the internal control systems are at the core of an organization, and they are important for the survival and sustained performance of a local NGO. The effectiveness of internal control practices will directly affect an NGO's overall sustainability.

Internal controls are a key management tool for assisting an NGO in its operational effectiveness and efficiency, maintenance of the integrity of available information, compliance with regulations, and financial reporting.

Local NGOs need to put in place proper internal control systems to help achieve accountability at all levels within the organization. This helps in resource allocation and risk management.

An internal control framework helps the organization follow a systematic approach in implementing a system of internal controls to support the NGO's operations and activities.

Internal control systems have two aspects: the control environment and the control procedures. The control environment includes management style, the NGO's culture, and a structure that provides support for effective internal control while the control procedures are summed up as entity-wide and process level controls, preventive and detective controls and finally manual and automated controls.

Organizations need to periodically determine the effectiveness of internal controls developed. This will assist management in understanding areas within the NGO that pose the greatest threat to achieving the mission if controls are not available or functioning effectively.

A local NGO's leadership and management must conduct periodic spot checks to ensure that adequate and relevant internal control policies and procedures are in place and enforced. This will help the team take appropriate actions to address risks that may hinder the performance and sustainability of the organization.

iii. ROBUST FUND MANAGEMENT PRACTICES

Funds are an important aspect in helping local NGOs undertake their programs and for overall management of the organization.

Sound grant management practices are becoming an important aspect because of the increasingly competitive nature of grant funding. Most local NGOs fail to effectively manage their funding because of;

a. poorly drafted project agreements or contracts,
b. poor project designs that lead to inadequate resources allocated to interventions,
c. recruitment of staff with low expertise,
d. ad hoc performance management system,
e. the failure to monitor and manage risks involved in contracts,
f. the failure to develop adequate organizational systems and processes, and
g. incomplete and inaccurate reporting.

Local NGOs that do not manage their grant funding well can easily lose credibility with stakeholders, and this can result in abrupt funding cuts. This affects the performance and overall survival of the organization.

It is important that NGOs are aware of the grant management cycle and understand the requirements of each phase for smooth management of funds. This helps an organization become more proactive in the management of mobilized resources.

CONCLUSION

The focus of most local NGOs has been mainly on the financial component of sustainability, and minimal focus has been on the other two components.

However, sustainability is not only about accessing funds for project implementation. It also requires the building of a steady and solid organization. This does not happen overnight but requires progressive steps toward a defined goal.

Many local NGOs find it difficult to progress toward organizational sustainability because they fail to effectively plan or measure their progress. Embarking on the implementation of initiatives that enhance sustainability is like turning a huge vessel, the key individuals steering can easily see the change, but the individuals at the rear of the vessel may not realize the change in position for a while.

An organization should identify and monitor key factors that influence its sustainability during the course of its existence. An NGO should have a clear view of the sustainability initiatives it needs and the behavior it wants to reinforce to develop into a high performance organization.

Planning and measuring progress toward sustained growth and performance is crucial and requires organizations to develop indicators to measure short- and long-term achievements.

This calls for a whole system approach to achieving organizational sustainability. A local NGO needs to plan for and monitor the following aspects to improve sustainability:

1. Determine the extent to which the NGO is planning for all the three components of sustainability. This requires developing a sustainability plan that highlights goals for all three components.(institutional, programmatic and financial).
2. Identify strategies to be adopted in the three aspects to address identified gaps or areas for improvement.
3. Identify delays or shortcomings in the selected strategies and plan for alternatives to minimize the obstacles.
4. Determine the adequacy of leadership and staff competencies to implement the initiatives.
5. Identify the available or required resources to support the initiatives.
6. Assess whether there is adequate and reliable information being gathered that shows the extent of achievement.
7. Periodically identify existing or potential organizational and external barriers that are hindering or may hinder sustainability initiatives.

An NGO's sustainability goals should, ideally, be aligned to its strategic priorities, and its operational and financial goals. A local NGO needs to continuously improve its management practices to meet its sustainability objectives. The sustainability efforts of the organization need to be in harmony with the targeted community capacities and stakeholders' interests.

An organization's chances of success increase when leadership actively strives to get feedback from other stakeholders and incorporates the feedback to develop sustainability strategies that are appropriate and responsive. An NGO's sustainability efforts are also affected by external factors like, the host country's policies or the development priorities of the host country or donors.

Chapter 7

THE PASSION TO EXCEL:
WHAT REALLY WORKS

When does an NGO realize it is performing poorly and that there is a need for a revamp to become a high performance organization? In some scenarios, the answer is straightforward for example, after an assessment conducted by a donor, or after new operations or a growth initiative. Other indicators may be difficult or subtle to monitor or notice because they are integrated into daily operations, for example, actions agreed upon not being implemented, or senior leadership spending less time focusing on strategic issues.

Too often, a well-established local NGO fails because its mission has gradually drifted away from the identified needs and expectations of its stakeholders. For an NGO to have sustained performance, it has to remain focused on donor priorities and stakeholder interests. At the same time, have a strong vision, strategic leadership and a responsive organizational structure and culture.

The level and extent to which an NGO will adopt the practices discussed in this book are affected by the organization's size, the nature of its operations or mandate, its structure and ownership characteristics, the complexity of its operations, and applicable laws and regulations.

Local NGOs that seek to be high performance organizations need to be adaptive and responsive by continuously identifying changes in the internal and external environment. They are also required to proactively develop strategies to exploit sector opportunities and minimize barriers to their success.

VALUE CREATION THROUGH BENCHMARKING PROCESS

Many local NGOs are faced with organizational inertia that prevents them from maximizing their potential or achieving sustained growth. Organizations need to be proactive in overseeing and measuring their performance.

Local NGOs that desire to be high-performance organizations need to be courageous and proactive enough to use the bench-marking method to explore and adopt best practices within their sector or from similar types of organizations so that they can have sustained performance.

Benchmarking entails making a comparison of an NGO's existing operations against those of its peers or competitors and identifying the improvements required to sustain performance and growth.

Benchmarking helps local NGOs to avoid the trap of "paradigm blindness" and it helps enhance organizational performance. Benchmarking approach requires organizations to identify the highest standards of excellence for services or processes within their sector or region of operation, and then develop actions to help realize those standards.

IMPORTANCE OF BENCHMARKING FOR LOCAL NGOs

Benchmarking helps NGOs to build a framework for excellence. The process of bench marking supports the organization to improve its processes or structures to consistently meet stakeholder expectations and keep the organization viable.

This process when effectively done can lead to discovery of new innovations or ideas for improving internal processes that assist an organization grow and sustain performance.

Benchmarking has the following benefits:

i. Increases productivity by helping organization minimize costs in execution while improving services or products.

    ii.   It reduces wastage of resources by identifying inefficient practices.

   iii.   It can be used as a strategic tool to jumpstart an organization that seemed stagnant by helping an organization map out where it is and where it desires to be.

   iv.   It helps promote creativity and learning among individuals and organizations as it assists in identification of new ideas by not only focusing on what is achieved but also the how.

    v.   It increases the potential for growth or expansion as the organization explores its external environment for new thinking.

   vi.   It helps build an organization's capabilities and competencies.

   vii.   It acts as an internal performance assessment tool both at individual and organizational level.

  viii.   It acts as a continuous and systematic improvement approach that enables the NGO set standards to improve processes.

   ix.   Increases stakeholders' satisfaction with NGO's performance.

The benchmarking process assists an organization build a team or workforce that continuously pursues excellence and enables an NGO be more responsive.

The benchmarking process should not be perceived as a quick fix solution for organizations. If no vision exists or continuous commitment to support the changes required then benchmarking will not bear any fruit or impact.

PROCESS OF BENCHMARKING

The bench marking practice is supported by a Hindu proverb that states, "Know the best to become the best."[40] It is a systematic process of exploration and discovery that enables an NGO embrace practices that lead to high performance.

It is an ongoing process that requires local NGOs to periodically question how the NGO processes measure against performance standards and adapting new practices or models that enable it gain and maintain a competitive excellence or edge. An organization can benchmark using the following steps;

1. Define and document the overall NGO's strategic objectives. The NGO has to ensure that benchmarking milestones are aligned to the NGO vision and mandate.
2. Explore and define what to benchmark (processes or systems, practices) by first understanding the organization's existing operations and improvements required.
3. Identify NGOs for comparison or an NGO it desires to learn from.
4. Form a team to oversee the process with the approval and commitment of the organization's leadership.
5. Create organization-wide interest and support for the process.
6. Collect and analyze the information.
7. Identify the transferable practices from the information collected. The practices or methods to be adopted by the NGO need to consider the prevailing circumstances within the organization. Make sure the benchmark process adopted is aligned to legal and ethical guidelines.
8. Develop objectives and indicators to measure the NGO's progress toward achieving the benchmarks.
9. Implement the agreed upon actions in a specified time schedule.
10. Measure progress to identify changes realized or the lack of changes. Identify barriers or enablers to the adoption of the new practices.
11. Redesign strategies to support implementation of the desired practices. The NGO requires a team that is committed and has the ability to analyze and make changes required.

The bench marking process can help NGOs identify opportunities for growth but unless action is taken to make changes required then the exercise is futile. Leaders often focus on the current deficiencies within an organization; however, a successful NGO should redesign itself to focus on available capitals to support its strategic priorities, minimize the organization's costs, and improve accountability.

Many NGOs sometimes focus more on the limitations that currently exist within the organization or get swayed by the seemingly urgent priorities of donors or complaints of frustrated teams. This however should not be the practice as it hinders an organization's capacity to grow.

A local NGO should be clear about what kind of organization it intends to build to achieve its envisioned mandates. The elements discussed in the preceding chapters are not static, as the development world keeps changing; therefore, local NGOs need to continuously adopt new ways of improving performance to continue surviving.

PURSUING SUSTAINABLE AND STRATEGIC ADVANTAGE

A local NGO must formulate internal and external strategies to support its development into a high performance organization. The NGO's leadership and management need to ask the following questions to assist them in developing strategies that will lead to high performance NGOs:

1. How close is the NGO to achieving effectiveness and self- sufficiency in its operations?
2. Does the NGO have an organizational and financial plan that includes targets for achieving effectiveness and self-sufficiency?
3. How will the NGO fund its operations for expansion or growth?
4. What structures and systems are in place to support the organization's plans to improve effectiveness and expansion?
5. How can the organization be restructured to accommodate growth and plans for self-sufficiency?
6. Do the management and organizational workforce have sufficient competencies and experience to respond and adapt to the NGO's growth and anticipated institutional challenges?
7. What is the NGO's niche and what opportunities exist?
8. What performance management and communication strategies are required?

A local NGO's effectiveness and sustainability are not entirely dependent on the resources that the entity mobilizes. They also depend on the entity's ability to establish enriching relations with stakeholders, strategic leadership, and successful management of change, adoption of new management practices and continuously monitoring the NGO's growth and performance.

It is crucial for an NGO to employ a sustainable approach for the growth and survival of the organization. However, not all organizations are seeking to adopt practices that would build their NGO effectiveness and sustainability.

Unfortunately, most local NGOs leave the growth of the organization to chance and this has resulted in many NGOs closing down their operations.

When an organization is competing for resources in a very tight market place the organization's appeal has to be different, better, cheaper and unique. A donor has no reason to select an NGO if there is no sign of innovativeness or value in supporting it.[41]

The management and leadership of many NGOs do not spend adequate time assessing the state of the organization. Developing a coherent strategy that enables an NGO to develop into a high performance organization is a good practice for an NGO that desires to grow.

Local NGOs in many developing nations are small and often lack easy access to the expert knowledge they need to build the organization. For example, they may realize that organizational learning is crucial, but have no clue how to undertake it.

Local NGOs operate in diverse ways within diverse cultural, social, political, and economic environments. A promising organizational practice in one country or organization may not necessarily be the best strategy in another. Therefore, it is important to contextualize each element, and that is what learning entails.

However, it is important for the leadership and management of local NGOs to understand that undertaking one single type or multiple types of change initiatives may not be sufficient to result in acceptable degrees of improvement in performance or sustainability. This is because organizations are different and respond differently to various stimuli during their lifecycles.

Therefore, embracing learning among local NGOs is crucial as it opens opportunities for continuous improvement in an organization's strategy, structures, and initiatives. An effective corporate culture accelerates the achievement of an NGO's strategic objectives. However, local NGOs need to understand that certain cultures are required at different organizational phases to support effective implementation of organizational strategic priorities.

Strategic positioning makes an organization effective, attractive, and sustainable. Strategic positioning defines the essence of who the organization is and what it does, and provides reasons why resource providers should support the NGO.

When it comes to elements that support organizational effectiveness and sustainability, there are no right or wrong strategies. Hence, it is up to each NGO to explore and review the options available and to choose the most appropriate mechanisms to enhance the organization's effectiveness and sustainability.

A local NGO will have difficulty in adopting practices to improve organizational effectiveness and sustainability if its leaders lack the competence to devise interventions that will ensure alignment between the strategy and overall organizational performance.

A high performance and sustainable NGO explores and selects strategies that are most appropriate to achieving its mission, to ensure the organization remains relevant year after year.

An organization that desires to excel, must ensure that its organizational structures, processes, and behavioral patterns are continually and totally aligned with the type of market the organization is designed to serve.[42]

Redesigning an organization toward achieving effectiveness and sustainability requires the integration of structures, processes, and people to support the implementation of strategy. Therefore, any redesign strategies must be tailored to the specific challenges, strengths, available assets, expertise, and change readiness of a given NGO.

Local NGOs require processes, structures, and practices that support the achievement of the mission of the organization through promoting a conducive environment where the employees accomplish their tasks. This allows the organization to be responsive to changing stakeholders' expectations and needs.

A local NGO needs to manage transitional risks as it adopts new organizational practices to improve its performance. Every change has potential risks such as interruptions to NGO's operations, employee retention, and poor implementation. NGOs need to mitigate the risks by identifying them early and monitoring them once the initiatives are adopted.

A local NGO that expands and thrives will do so because it has envisioned, and designed strategies to embrace a future that looks different from its present or past. In addition, the NGO is willing to respond to changes and seize new opportunities within its operating environment to improve performance.

END NOTES

INTRODUCTION

1. Carmen Malena, *Working with NGOs: A Practical Guide to Operational Collaboration between the World Bank and Nongovernmental Organizations* (Washington, DC: World Bank, 1995), Last Modified September 15, 2014, http://documents.worldbank.org/curated/en/1995/03/697561/working-ngos-practical-guide-operational-collaboration-between-world-bank-nongovernmental-organizations

2. Keith Owen, Ron Mundy, Wil Guild and Robert Guild (2001) *Creating and sustaining the high performance organization.* http://citeseerx.ist.psu.edu/viewdoc/download;jsessionid=3D08E648D746349DA6F20B671DDF29C8?doi=10.1.1.472.3780&rep=rep1&type=pdf Last modified on October 29, 2015

CHAPTER ONE

3. Hillarie Owen *New Thinking on Leadership: Global perspective.* London. Kogan Page.2012, Pg 13 Last modified on 2/March /2014

4. John Eric Adair *The John Adair Lexicon of Leadership.*The Definitive guide to Leadership Skills and Knowledge. (London. Kogan 2011:92) Last modified March 2,2014

5. Owen, *New Thinking*, 96,

CHAPTER TWO

6. Murray E.Jennex, *Knowledge Management in Modern Organizations* (Hershey, PA: Idea Group Publication, 2007, 52.

7. Jennex, *Knowledge Management in Modern Organizations*,3

8. Kimiz Dalkir, *Knowledge Management in Theory and Practice* (Cambridge, MA: MIT Press, 2011), 2.

9. Dalkir, *Knowledge Management in Theory and Practice*, 32.

10. Knowledge Connections"Developing Qualifying Elements for Strategic Transformation". http://www.kconnections.com.my/neuquest.html. Last modified on March,11-2015

11. Dalkir, *Knowledge Management in Theory and Practice*, 21.

CHAPTER THREE

12. Project Management Institute, Inc (2013) PMI's Pulse of the Profession The High Cost of Low Performance. The Essential Role of Communications, May 2013. Pg 5.Last modified March 7th 2015
http://www.pmi.org/-/media/pmi/documents/public/pdf/learning/thought-leadership/pulse/the-essential-role-of-communications.pdf

13. Joep Cornelisson, *Corporate Communication. A Guide to Theory and Practice* (Hampshire: Ashford Colour Press, 2011), 5.

14. Paolo Mefalopulos,(2008) *Development Communication Source Book. Broadening the Boundaries of Communication* (Washington, DC: International Bank for Reconstruction and Development/ The World Bank, 2008), 26. http://siteresources.worldbank.org/ EXTDEVCOMMENG/Resources/DevelopmentCommSourcebook. pdf. Last Modified June 6, 2014,

15. Cornelisson, *Corporate Communication*, 81.

16. Project Management Institute, Inc, Communication. The Message is clear. December 2013 http://www.pmi.org/-/media/pmi/documents/public/pdf/white-papers/communications.pdf. December 2013,Pg 2,Last modified August 2016

17. PMI, Inc, Communication. The Message is clear. Pg 2

18. Mefalopulos, *Development Communication Source Book.* 155.

19. PMI, Inc. Essential Role of Communications, Pg 2

CHAPTER FOUR

20. Batti, R. C. (2015), Development Project Management Within Local NGOs: 10 Recommendations to Meet 10 Challenges. Global Bus and Org Exc, 34: 21–29. http://onlinelibrary.wiley.com/doi/10.1002/joe.21623. Last modified July 2015

21. Sanjay Mehta, *Enterprise Risk Management: Insights and Operationalization* (Morristown, N.J: Financial Executives Research Foundation, 2010), 3

22. Mehta, *Enterprise Risk Management,* 5

CHAPTER FIVE

23. Rachel Blackman, *Organizational Governance,* Roots 10 (Teddington: Tearfund, 2006), 5. http://tilz.tearfund.org/-/media/Files/TILZ/Publications/ROOTS/English/Governance/ROOTS%2010%20E.pdf. Last modified March 15, 2015

24. Wendy MacDonald, *Board Building: Recruiting and Developing Effective Boards*, pg. 3. https://www.muttart.org/wp-content/uploads/2015/11/Recruiting-and-Development-2008.pdf. Last modified on August 8, 2015

25. MacDonald, *Board Building*,3

26. MacDonald, *Board Building*, 16

27. MacDonald, *Board Building*, 13

28. Blackman, *Organizational Governance*, 5

CHAPTER SIX

29. Owen, Mundy, Guild and Guild, *Creating and Sustaining the High Performance Organization*, 11

30. Richard Woodman, William Pasmore, and Abraham Shani, *Research in Organization Change and Development* (Bingley: Emerald, 2011). 80

31. Woodman, Pasmore and Shani :14

32. Rehema C. Batti (2014), "Human Resource Management Challenges Facing Local NGOs." *Humanities and Social Sciences,* Vol. 2, No. 4, 2014, pp. 87–95. Online. Last modified August 27, 2015.

33. Michael Armstrong (2012),Armstrong's Handbook of Human Resource Management Practice. Kogan Page.UK.16

34. Batti, *"Human Resource Management Challenges."*

35. J. Kociatkiewicz and D. Jemielniak, *Handbook of Research on Knowledge Intensive Organizations*, E-book (Hershey, PA: Information Science Reference, 2009), 5 Last Modified June 10,2014

36. Miltiadis Lytras, Mier Russ, Ronald Maier, Amborjorn Naeve, *Knowledge Management Strategies: A Handbook of Applied Technologies.* (Hershey:IGI Publishing, 2008), 194.

37. Jennex, *Knowledge Management*, 4.

38. Rehema C. Batti (2014), "Challenges Facing Local NGOs in Resource Mobilization". Humanities and Social Sciences. Vol. 2, No. 3, pp. 57-64. [Online].

39. Susan DiMattia, "Getting the Money You Need: Relationship Fundraising." Online. January 2008; 32(1) 26. Last modified on March 30, 2014.

CHAPTER SEVEN
40. Dalkir *Knowledge Management in Theory and Practice*,348

41. Batti, *Challenges Facing Local NGOs in Resource Mobilization*

42. Owen, Mundy, Guild and Guild, 12